Impossible
With Men

"Happy Days
Your Friend,
John Wilson."

John Wilson

with
James McClelland

AMBASSADOR

Belfast • Greenville

Ambassador Publications
a division of
Ambassador Productions Ltd.
Providence House
Ardenlee Street,
Belfast,
BT6 8QJ
Northern Ireland
www.ambassador-productions.com

Emerald House
427 Wade Hampton Blvd.
Greenville
SC 29609, USA
www.emeraldhouse.com

CONTENTS

JOHN WILSON AND FAMILY

For my wife and daughter
Carole and Rebekah.
True loves.

For all my brothers
and sisters in Christ.
I love you all.

For the world I once knew.
Jesus loves you.
John 3 v16.

Chapter One

IN THE SLAMMER AGAIN

W ell John, back again, eh?" The familiar voice seemed almost
sympathetic. After the briefest of pauses, the same old routine began again.

How I hated prison reception! Prison sentences themselves were
quite easy now. I'd done so many I was used to them. But no matter
how many times I'd been "inside" I'd never got used to the prison
reception procedure. I always found it an unbearable hassle.

In Brixton prison, where I'd served a few times, it takes up to eight
hours from stepping through those forbidding front gates till the cell
door finally clangs behind you. But this time it was the local jail in
Dumfries and a procedure lasting only two to three hours.

Four months - for stabbing an Alsatian dog! That's what I was being
banged up for. Even I could hardly believe it, but it was true. This was
my tenth prison sentence in eight years. A catalogue of thirty-seven
previous convictions lay behind me. The crimes ranged from robbery
to attempted murder.

"Right Wilson!" the guard ordered, "Get stripped for the doctor's
inspection." I did so quickly, wrapping a towel around the lower half of
my body before stepping into the tiny cubicle referred to as "the dog
box."

REFLECTION

Sitting there, awaiting the doctor's examination, I began to think seriously about my life. To say it was a bit of a mess is an understatement.

"How many more times will my freedom be taken from me?" I thought. Then a voice from within retorted, "What freedom?"

Sadly, it was true. I never really did feel free. Even when I wasn't in prison I felt bound up. Where had it all gone wrong? Every sentence I had ever done had been someone else's fault, or so I had maintained. But now I was getting tired of pretending to myself, even though I kept pretending that, really, I couldn't help the way I was made.

YOU AGAIN WILSON!

"Ah, it's you again!" The sudden roar of the prison doctor's voice woke me from my sorrowful reverie. "Bend over," he barked, and over I went. "Now straighten up," he barked again. He shone a light down my front. "OK," he said "He's clean."

"Any pains, wooden legs, glass eyes, hooks instead of hands, wigs, false ears .... Well? ... Well?" He was fast loosing patience.

"Yes," I said, "I've got two special fitments for my feet and I'd like to request my own boots."

"Request granted. Get dressed!" Once more he barked his commands like a sergeant major. "Get dressed," meant donning the prison clothing. Shirt too tight, trousers too slack, jacket with no buttons, pants and vest like bell tents, socks of different colours. "Ah well," I thought, "Who cares?"

A SCARECROW

There I stood, like a tidy scarecrow, prison pack in front of me, waiting to be marched over to the main prison wing.

Because of my bad feet I was given a ground floor cell. At least I was being afforded a modicum of mercy.

The cell door clanged shut behind me and the key rattled in the lock. These sounds were so familiar that they hardly bothered me anymore. I proceeded to make up the bed with sheets which were too short, then lay back on it to roll a cigarette.

A prison cell isn't the most interesting of places and so, as I lay there, I studied the back of the cell door. I'd seen it all before and knew it off by heart. Hobbs & Co. London SE11 had made the prison door, a heavy, thick metal object securely held together all the way around with nuts and bolts. I didn't bother to count them. I already knew there were thirty-nine.

HOW LONG?

Again my mind drifted off in pitiful reverie. What was to become of me? How long can I keep this up - in and out of prison with monotonous regularity? I had lost the fight and no-one had to tell me where the weakness was. The truth was, I was a slave - to drink.

Getting up from the bed I stepped to where the mirror was screwed to the wall. The sight that gazed back at me from that mirror was so pitiful. My face was black and blue. There were two big bumps on my head and when I looked down at my hands, there was a big open gash on my right thumb.

Here I was, twenty-seven years of age, and a complete slave to drink and drugs. Why did it have to be this bad? Hadn't I had enough?

Well, I had three more days in this local clink before being moved on to Barlinnie prison in Glasgow. I knew it well, I'd been there six times before. But, as I say, I had three more days to reflect on the circumstances and events which had brought me to this pitiful point in my short life. Would I ever be delivered from this mess?

Chapter Two

HOME SWEET HOME!

Thank you gentlemen," my dad said to the ambulance-men and waved them goodbye. I stood there in front of my father, trembling and very frightened. At ten years of age, I had just been fished out of the salmon hole where I had almost drowned. A lorry driver spotted my predicament and his quick and courageous action saved my life.

Now, sitting in the kitchen of my home in Dumfries, I gradually began to feel physically better. But my father's reaction to the events did nothing to encourage my spirits.

As my mother made the supper my father lectured me. "Don't see why you can't be more careful," he intoned. "And I hope you don't think you're staying off school because of this?"

"No dad." I was in no position to argue.

"All right then, finish your supper and get off to bed!"

My bedroom was the attic. It was my refuge from the storms of life. That a lad of ten years should need such a refuge is probably unthinkable but in my case it was necessary.

THAT AGE OLD CURSE!

My mum and dad were good to me, as good as they could be. But there were problems, and sadly they too had an association with drink and the abuse of it.

My father had a taxi business and earned good money. My mother worked as the head waitress at the local Station Hotel. So we weren't poor by any means. But it takes more than money and what it can buy to give a boy a good and happy childhood.

Saturday nights were the problem and they instilled in me an almost constant dread. My mum and dad went out on Saturday nights leaving me in the care of my older brother. He was fourteen.

By the time my mum and dad arrived home I would be in bed and right down below the covers. At about two o'clock in the morning my parents would come in, well under the influence of drink. Usually there would be a couple of friends along with them.

Upstairs in my bed I'd be praying that they wouldn't disturb me. But they usually did. Saturday night after Saturday night my mother came into my room, woke me up and brought me downstairs to meet the visitors.

Down in the big room my dad would have the record player on, with Frank Sinatra belting out "Chicago," and he trying to compete at the top of his voice.

FAMILY WARS

I was paraded in front of the strangers, given a couple of shillings and then bundled back up to bed again. It was only a matter of time till the trouble began. Bumps, thuds and bangs came from the big room. Next, the sound of a record smashing. Then a window. It sounded like bedlam downstairs.

Next morning, Sunday, mum would be sporting a black eye and a burst lip. Dad would have scratches and cuts on his face. I couldn't understand why they went through this misery every week-end. How could a Saturday night's so called entertainment turn into scenes like this?

SUNDAY MORNINGS

One Sunday morning I came down to the kitchen to much the same scene as on every other week. Both mum and dad had the usual marks of fighting and the atmosphere was so morbid even a lad of my tender years could feel it.

"You have gone too far this time," my mother blurted out. "Look at my face! I'm leaving you for good!"

"Don't be stupid woman," my dad retorted. "When are you going to grow up?"

With that there was the crash of an ornament smashing right beside my father and then a string of oaths and curses. Saturday night's drink still hadn't worn off.

LEAVING AGAIN

At the top of the stairs the three suitcases were already packed. Yes my mum was leaving - again. She had done so about ten times before but always came back.

Every time she left home I was asked which of them I wanted to go with, mum or dad. Usually I went with my mother, over to her sister, my aunt. This arrangement never lasted long and after a week or so my mother and I would be back home again. Trouble is, I loved them both very much and just like any other boy, wanted us all to be together as one happy family.

On this particular Sunday morning, as my mother threatened to leave, I decided that I couldn't endure the situation anymore. I had to escape from the fear, the uncertainty, the heartache and the agony that was tearing me apart.

RUNNING AWAY

In frustration I screamed at them both. I said I hated them for being so horrible and then, as quickly as it takes to tell this, I was out the front door, round to the back of the house, over the wall into the garden next door and away.

I ran and ran until it seemed my lungs would burst, but never stopped to rest. Eventually I hit the main road out of town and headed south. There was no need to run now, I was well away from home.

After walking for about three miles, I came to a spot on the road where a stream flowed under a small bridge. It was a scorching summer and by now I was weary and exhausted with the heat. The little bridge seemed an ideal place to shelter and well out of the way of suspicious eyes. In a moment I had hopped the fence, slithered down the bank and was in below the bridge out of sight.

REFLECTIONS

Once sat down, the trauma of the whole situation overwhelmed me. Sitting there underneath that little bridge, with my knees gathered up to my chest, my entire emotions burst forth in a flood of tears. Afraid, exhausted, confused and sorry for myself, I sat there weeping for hours. I wondered how many other little boys of ten were in circumstances like mine.

Weeping did nothing to relieve the turmoil. Indeed, it worsened as I reflected on what I had blurted out to my mother and father that morning as I ran from the house.

I didn't hate them at all. In fact I loved them dearly. I just wanted for us to be a normal happy family and I couldn't understand why were weren't.

A NEW LIFE

I'd ran from the house at about ten o'clock that morning. It was now early afternoon. What would I do? What could I do? I certainly couldn't go back home again. Then the answer came. I would go to England and start a whole new life - at ten years of age!

Scrambling back up the bank and onto the road I resumed my walk south. My plan was to hitch a lift but that was where the scheme began and finished. What I would do when I got to England hadn't even entered my head. I had no idea where I would stay or what I would live on. I had no money either. As it happened, I never did get much time to think about these things.

My confused thoughts were suddenly shocked into sharp focus by the sight of a police car. I instinctively knew they were looking for me and decided to make a run for it. Over the fence I leapt and across the field. A glance back showed the police car stopped by the roadside and the officers already in pursuit.

PANIC!

Blind panic seized me now. I stumbled onward determined to escape. However, there was no hope of out-running the policemen. Each time I glanced backwards they were narrowing the gap. Then a hand on my shoulder, a tightening grip and a soft, comforting voice.

It's all right son. Calm down now. Nobody wants to harm you." The policeman was as nice as he could be.

"Now what's your name son? Are you John Wilson? Your mum and dad are worried sick about you and we've been searching for you for hours. Come on, we'll take you home."

Although one part of me wanted to go back to the comfort of my own room, I begged them not to take me home. I was afraid of what mum and dad would say to me. Afraid, too, of next Saturday morning and a repeat of what had happened today. But of course I agreed to go and was driven home in the front seat of the police car.

I cried openly when the policemen handed me over to my mother. I cried out of relief that the events of the morning were over, but I cried, too, because my mother, once again, was sporting a big black eye.

When the police left, mum and dad gave me lots of hugs and kisses - and promised never to fight again. That night I went up to bed feeling better than I had in a long time, indeed, better than I could remember.

Chapter Three

THE YOUNG CELEBRITY!

O n the Monday morning after the incident at the salmon hole I awoke with a happy heart. In a few minutes I was up, dressed and downstairs for breakfast. I ate heartily, the new found joy giving me a man sized appetite.

Mum was even more pleasant than usual, attending to my every need and wishing me well for school. She handed me my dinner money for the week and an extra half-crown for the National Savings Certificates. Savings Certificates were a big thing in those days - to instil into children the wisdom of thrift. After a final hug and good-bye I was away over the hill to St. Michael's primary school.

In the mornings it took me about five minutes to get to school. Coming home took about an hour. There was always some diversion along the way for a ten year old boy and there was usually another ten year old around to help him find those diversions.

What a surprise awaited me when I returned home on this first day after my swimming accident. My father sat in the living room and there were two strange men with him. He explained they were from the local newspaper and that they'd heard about my dice with death a couple of days ago. They wanted to hear the whole story - and they wanted a photograph too! Suddenly I felt like some kind of hero.

FAME

With as much graphic detail as my young and fertile mind could muster I told the horrific account of my miraculous escape from the jaws of death.

I had dived into the river and begun the swim across to the far side. Halfway across, however, where the water is deepest and the current very strong, I had suddenly been seized with a terrible cramp in my side. Powerless to go on and helpless against the strength of the current, I began to go under. I panicked so much I could barely shout for help. All I could manage were a few feeble croaks.

Fortunately, a lorry driver was standing near the spot where I was thrashing about in the water. He spotted my predicament and without thought for his own safety, jumped fully clothed into the water and dragged me out.

The newspaper seemed impressed by my account of events and made suitable noises of surprise and awe as the story unfolded. What a lucky escape I'd had and what a brave boy to be able to re-tell the story so well.

WATCH THE BIRDIE!

Then it was time for the picture. "Nip upstairs son." Dad had sat quietly as I told my story but now, perhaps feeling slightly proud of me, he wanted to make sure his wee son looked his best for the photograph. "Wet and comb your hair and put a clean jersey on," he called after me.

When the picture and story appeared in Saturday morning's "Standard," I was a right proud lad. However, my euphoria was to be short lived. Next Saturday night mum and dad went out, as usual and came home the following morning, as usual - plastered. In the early hours of Sunday I was under the bed covers again, sobbing my heart out. Their promise was broken. It's a blunt statement to make, but it was a blunt reality.

In an effort to drown my sorrows I decided to fill every spare moment of my life with fun and pleasure. For me, just a boy of ten, that meant spending as much time as possible with my pals, playing in the street. Chief of these pals was Cliff, three years my senior and the street baddie.

DOWNHILL AGAIN

We disappeared for whole days at a time, swimming in the river, bird nesting, "rumping" apples, or playing amongst the old, wrecked cars dumped down in the quarry.

Once, when playing in the dump, Cliff nearly lost his life. We were killing the rats that infested the place and on this occasion I was standing with a long pole poking at the rubbish when a rat scurried out. It was as big as a six month old kitten and when Cliff spied it he threw a lemonade bottle at it. He missed, and he and I chased after it across the dump.

We were just about to follow it through a barbed wire fence when, behind me, I heard Cliff yelling in panic. Wheeling round I could see that he was stuck - and sinking into a pool of black, oily mire.

"Get me out," he cried in desperation. "I don't want to die."

DESPERATION

I took his hand and heaved with all my childish might but it was no good. He was stuck fast. I ran back to the dump and grabbed the pole I had been using to poke at the rats. When I got back to Cliff he was in to his waist and was still going down. There was nothing I could do, even with the pole.

Over in a nearby football field a group of older boys were in the middle of a friendly match. I shouted and screamed at them, panicking for Cliff who seemed certain to be done for. Thankfully the big lads came running to see what the fuss was about. By this time all that was showing of Cliff was his shoulders and his head.

The big lads managed to get hold of him and drag him to safety. He was in so deep, however, and the slimy pool had such a hold on him that it took a long time. When they eventually got him out he was a sorry mess, black from head to foot, and stinking. He breathed some heavy sighs of relief when delivered from what seemed certain death.

A CLOSE SHAVE

Shortly after this I had a very close shave with death myself. Coming out of the cinema after a Saturday morning matinee my mind was still on the excitement of the film I'd just seen. Road safety codes didn't even enter my head as I thoughtlessly dashed across the street in the path of a car. The driver didn't have a chance and when the car hit me I was catapulted up over the bonnet and on to the roof, from whence I fell with a thud on the pavement.

Terrified, naturally, by what had happened I burst into a fit of hysterical screaming and it took my brother's constant slapping of my face to shock me out of it.   I, too, had been spared.

Chapter Four

THE HARD MAN

A t the age of twelve I moved up from primary to the secondary school. At this time my home life wasn't so bad - at least I'd become used to my parents' feuding, or had hardened myself to it.

Both my older brothers had made names for themselves as "hard men," so I took their lead and adopted the worldly philosophy of "every man for himself." It was a philosophy which was to lead me on a path of destruction.

"Small oaks from little acorns grow," goes the old saying and it can be applied to many aspects of life. Around this time I was to plant a little acorn of wickedness which over the next few years would grow into a mighty oak tree. In such a simple way my life of crime had its beginnings.

One week-end, my friend Cliff, another older boy, and myself went for a swim in the river. At a spot where some other boys had left their clothes to go swimming as well, we hatched a plan. We would creep along the bank to where their clothes were laid, rifle the pockets and steal whatever we could find

THE LAW AGAIN

We had just relieved the clothing of a few pounds, some rings and watches and a medallion when the alarm was sounded. An older boy appeared from nowhere and began shouting to his friends that their property was being stolen.

We took to our heels in blind panic, running just anywhere to escape capture. However, captured we were. The police were called and after questioning we were bundled into the Land Rover and taken to my home.

The sequel to the whole incident was that Cliff and the other lad were charged with theft. I was warned not to get involved in anything of the like again. It should have been a lesson to me - but of course it wasn't.

AMBITION

My one great ambition in life was to play football. Ever since primary school I had almost lived for the game. The class work I hated, the football I loved. At school I played centre forward and had also played for Dumfries Select, a team made up from all the schools in South West Scotland.

When I went to High School my great ambition was to play for the team and this I did in the first year. However, my soccer career was brought to an abrupt end one day in the school gymnasium. Another lad and I got into a fight and since he was much bigger than me, although of the same age, I felt I had to resort to something more than bare fists to get the better of him.

There was a javelin propped against the wall and when I broke free I grabbed it. It would appear that everyone else in the gym realised that I fully intended to "stick" the other guy with the javelin for they scattered left and right and scaled the wall bars like monkeys.

To escape my wrath, the boy I'd been fighting with ran to the other end of the gym. This infuriated me even more. I threw the javelin after him with such force that it stuck, like an arrow, in the wooden vaulting horse, just missing him.

Of course the alarm was raised and the teachers ran in. I was apprehended and duly punished with a few lashes of the strap. But worse than that - much worse - I was dropped from the soccer team.

TOTAL REBELLION

For me, this was the last straw. Any chance of me settling down to live within the bounds of the normal rules of society was gone. As far as I was concerned it was now all-out war with authority - outright rebellion against every form of law and order. There would be no more doing what others wanted; no more bowing to convention; no more doing what was expected of me.

The summer holidays came and by now, I was thirteen years old. Another friend of mine "Stu" and myself, went swimming near the boat-house. After a time, Stu left the water and got dressed again. I decided to stay in a while longer. Perhaps I stayed in for too long because, suddenly, I was seized by cramp and realised that I was in difficulty.

My cries for help were ignored by Stu. In fact he thought I was making fun and just sat there laughing at my plight. Even when I was going down for the third time he showed no concern. He didn't go for help. He didn't even raise the alarm.

To be truthful, we were both to blame for this. In the past, when swimming, we had often cried out for help in jest. Now when there was a genuine emergency, Stu thought this was just another case of "Wolf! wolf!"

TERROR

As I went down for what I thought was the last time, the whole of my short life flashed before me. For some reason my thoughts were of my grandmother. Then blackness descended - and oblivion.

Consciousness gradually returned and the mists began to clear. I was on the bank, with an old man above me, squeezing the water out of my lungs. It was the boatman. He had a hut nearby and purely by chance, or perhaps I should say, by providence, he looked out of the small window just in time to see me going under.

He dashed out, clambered into a boat and using his hands as oars propelled the boat out to where I was sinking. He wasn't a moment too soon, for my head was already below the water. However, he found me, grabbed my hair and pulled me up and out.

As we sat together in his little hut, sipping some of his hot tea, he asked my name. "John Scott," I replied, being afraid to give him my real name in case he would tell my dad. Afterwards I thought, "The man has just saved my life and I have the effrontery to lie to him."

ETERNAL REALITIES!

Later that evening, in the comfort of my bedroom, the full import of what had happened came home to me with force. What if I had died? Where would I have spent eternity. It didn't take long to dismiss these morose thoughts for I reasoned that heaven would have been my destination. After all, didn't God love everybody? Hell was just for really wicked people - like murderers - and Hitler!

At home, life was quite bearable through the week. However, the constant week-end drinking sprees undermined any trust I ever had in my parents.

As well as the regular week-end sessions my dad used to go drinking mid-week as well. One of his mates usually joined him and they ended up in our house just at about the time I got home from school. On days like these, coming home was like facing an assault mission. I never knew who, or what I'd meet.

One occasion in particular sticks out in my mind. I'd just come in from school, mid-week, and dad was there with one of his cronies. They'd just come back from the pub and must have had a right few jars.

HOME ABUSE AGAIN

As soon as I stepped through the door my dad started to scold me. He was determined to make a big issue out of something which was really very small. In hindsight, what he was going on about doesn't matter a jot. Anyway, the scolding continued and ended up with him cuffing me on the ear. However, what was even worse was that his cronie slapped me as well. This really hurt me. Not physically - I was well used to getting the odd cuff around the ear - but deep inside I was hurt. How could a father allow another man to beat his own son? I really hated my dad for this.

My mother, too, was a troubled soul. She worked very hard throughout the week, but Saturday nights found her, as usual at the pub living it up.

The rows and fights between her and dad continued regularly and often with great ferocity. She was so distressed by it all that, on several occasions, she tried to take her own life by overdosing on tablets.

Again and again the ambulance would scream up to our house and whisk my mum off to hospital to have her stomach pumped out. All this distressed me no end and I used to do a lot of crying for her, wishing with all my heart that life could be different.

That was the tragic reality of life in our home - and for me. However, when anyone outside asked me about my home life I lied about it, making out that we were all very happy.

All have sinned and come short of the glory of God.

Romans 3:23

Chapter Five

New Beginnings

Just as I was approaching my fourteenth birthday we moved to a new house. By this time my two older brothers had left home. They had had enough of the miserable circumstances we all endured and decided to step out on their own and survive as best they could. There was a great lack of security in the family. In fact, there wasn't any. I suppose that's why my brothers bailed out for good. They had lost the determination to see it through; to try and make a go of family life.

The new house was much smaller but with only mum, dad and myself now that wasn't going to be a problem. Indeed, there was a great sense of a new beginning for us. Perhaps from now peace and harmony would descend upon our family.

For a thousand other families in the same situation there would have been perfect peace and harmony. There was no excuse for us. We were well blessed with material goods. As well as his taxi business, my father had a shop which did very well. It was, he said, like having a licence to print money.

He bought and sold watches, cameras, binoculars, bicycles, rings, record-players, transistor radios and such like. The turnover was steady and the profits were good. So we weren't poor. My mum worked too - a part time job in a factory. But she did it only for the sake of passing the time. She didn't need the money.

In material goods we were comfortable, indeed, well off. But as far as the inward possessions of peace, satisfaction, contentment and true love, we had nothing. We were paupers!

ALEX AND GUS

By the time I was fourteen I had a couple of part time jobs with two men who were brothers. One was a fish buyer, the other a scrap metal dealer. Each of the two men was a character in his own way and life with them was never dull. I had one or two narrow escapes in their company.

Alex was their van driver and once, when he and I were driving home after a delivery, we almost came a cropper on the highway.

His little Volkswagen Beetle was buzzing along merrily and Alex and I were having a good old chin wag when suddenly one of the back wheels came off and went trundling past us. The car lurched to one side as the corner without the wheel dropped to the tarmac. Then it began to swerve from side to side as Alex, oaths and curses pouring from him, fought to keep it under control.

Just above the glove compartment there was a hand grip. I grasped it with both hands and hung on tight.

As the rear hub scraped along the ground, a fierce grinding sound from the rear hub almost drowned out the engine noise and showers of multi-coloured sparks flew high into the air.

After what seemed like an age Alex managed to get the car down to a controllable speed and then brought it to a halt. It took us about five minutes to regain enough composure to walk back up the road and re-trieve the missing wheel.

KEYSTONE COPS

On another occasion Gus, the other brother, and I were touring around farms looking for old machinery to buy as scrap. The roads around the Galloway hills are narrow and winding, not designed for speeds above about thirty miles per hour.

Gus went into a bend at about fifty miles an hour and then realised we weren't going to make it out the other end. In panic he let go of the wheel and the car careered headlong into a stone dyke and halfway through it.

It was just like a scene from a Keystone Cops movie. There we were, still in the car, balanced precariously over the centre of the dyke. Behind us - the roadway. In front - a seventy foot drop!

Thankfully we had the presence of mind to sit still till the car stopped teetering. Then, very carefully, we clambered into the back to shift the weight. I managed to scramble out through a window. Gus took a chance and opened the door. We were shaken but safe.

Lying there in the middle of the road, reflecting on our narrow escape and wondering what to do about the van, we heard a familiar whining sound. It was Sindy, Gus' pet dog. She was still in the van, cowering under the front seat. Slowly and carefully Gus climbed back into the van and just managed to retrieve the dog before the van took another lunge forward. It stuck though.

RESCUE

My ankle was sprained and I was in a lot of pain so Gus went for help. About half an hour later I heard the familiar snore of a tractor engine approaching. It was Gus, with a neighbouring farmer who had come to the rescue. Ropes were attached to the van and after a bit of scraping and crunching, as the tractor hauled it off the dyke, it was back on the roadway again.

It didn't take a very close inspection to assess the damage. The whole front end had been driven in by the force of the impact. The mudguards and bumper were stuck fast against the front wheels so that they wouldn't turn. The headlamps were smashed and the windscreen was a million pieces of splintered glass. It was no more.

Gus and the farmer set too with hammers and re-arranged the bodywork to make the van driveable again. Then, somewhat subdued, we were on our way home. However, the excitement for that day wasn't over just yet.

About two miles from Dumfries we were just about to overtake a racing bike ridden by a young lad of about my age. Suddenly the bike swerved, then wobbled, then crashed just in front of us.

We stopped to help, gathering up the boy who had injured his arm. The bike was in an even sorrier state than our van. So we slung it into the back, took the boy on board, and headed on for Dumfries. It must have been a rather sorry sight that eventually struggled into town that evening. A wrecked van, a mangled bike and a trio of shattered individuals.

MY FIRST DRINK

I used to attend a local youth club in the town and one night when I came home my mum and dad were having one of their parties. These parties, with lots of friends and cronies invited, usually started off rather quietly but almost always ended up in near chaos.

One of my dad's friends turned to me and asked me to finish his drink because he was driving. My dad was well on by this time and I was fairly sure he wouldn't catch on, so I took it and downed it one gulp. It tasted absolutely awful, like perfume I thought. I discovered later it was neat gin.

However, since it didn't seem to have any immediate effect I was perfectly happy to oblige my dad's friend and finish his drinks for the rest of the evening. Dad kept pouring them. His friend kept passing them to me and I continued to finish them, with the result that after five or six of these neat potions I was hopelessly drunk.

Well of course the source of my illicit supply was eventually discovered and when it was, it gave everybody a good chuckle. Nobody thought it disgraceful that a child should have been given enough drink to make a fool both of him and his parents. It was all a great source of amusement. Thinking on this event today I'm reminded of the words from the Bible "Fools make a mock of sin."

I was packed off to bed with hardly a word been said. Certainly there was no condemnation of my folly or stupidity. Being drunk, of course, I slept very quickly and very soundly. However, next morning I was to pay the price for my wickedness. For the first time in my life I experienced the horror of a hangover and had to stay in bed all day nursing it. I was so ill I couldn't even think of going to school. I don't think I could have made it anyway. I did spend the day, though, promising myself that alcohol would never cross my lips again. How often since then have I wished that my promise had been kept.

Chapter Six

INTRODUCTION TO A CELL

Halfway through my fourteenth year my mate Dandy and myself embarked on a series of daring break-ins. We carefully planned and targeted certain shops and houses where we knew the pickings would be good. Over a period of three months we took money, cigarettes, clothing and drink, most of which we sold on the black market. We kept the odd bottle of wine on which we quickly got drunk and spent the money on dances, picture shows and girls. At just over fourteen years of age we were sampling our idea of the high life and we loved it.

By the time we had come to the end of the three months the local papers were carrying stories of "The phantom robbers," whose specialist trade mark was the ability to enter premises through very small windows.

Carelessness brought our brilliant run of success to a swift conclusion. A police patrol came across Dandy lying drunk in an entry one night. Being drunk was only a small problem. The give away was the large sum of money stuffed in his pockets.

I was standing a short distance away when the police found Dandy. Instead of keeping quiet I shouted abuse at them, telling them to leave him alone. It didn't take them long to catch me too and then both of us were given a ride in a big car - to the police station.

At the police station we were subjected to hours of questioning. Naturally, the truth came out and we ended up with seven charges of house breaking plus a charge of theft. Because we were so young we were allowed to share the same cell but that didn't make it anymore enjoyable.

My mother came to see me, told me not to worry, pressed her head up close to the food hatch to give me a kiss on the cheek and then left. I think she was more worried than I was. Of course, she had plenty of her own worries and fears, especially the fear of my dad.

ESCAPE!

Dandy and I squeezed up together on the single mattress and began to think. We pretended not be in the least bothered about what had happened to us. Then, jokingly, one of us said "Why don't we escape?"

We thought about it for a while and then decided to investigate the possibility further. Dandy stuck his head out through the food hatch, had a look around and reported that the top gate of the cell block had been left open. Well, after all, this wasn't death row or a maximum security wing.

Looking at the open hatch, very small and a fair height above the floor, we concluded that escape was out of the question. Then we looked at it again - and thought it might just be a possibility.

I lifted Dandy up as high as I could and he very soon wriggled his way through the tiny opening. It was a kind of scary moment when he stood on one side of the jail's iron barred door and I stood on the other.

Then it was my turn. How I managed to scramble up high enough to get my head and shoulders through the open food hatch I'll never know. I did, though, and then Dandy tugged and hauled until my whole body was through and I stood beside him - grinning from ear to ear. The bruised rib I got in the process was hardly felt.

COMMANDOS

Putting on our shoes we tip-toed to the end of the corridor and peeped through the chink in the partly open door. A police sergeant sat at a desk typing out a pile of reports. His back was turned at an angle to us and he was so intent on the task on hand that he never saw or heard us creeping past him. A half open window enticed us to greater boldness and, like a scene from a commando movie, we slipped out on to the sill and dropped to the yard below. Thankfully, no one either saw or heard us.

We were on the ground beside a "Black-Maria." A few yards away the gates to the station's vehicle entrance lay wide open. With furtive looks in every direction we crept the short distance to the gates, peeked our heads around the corner, saw that the coast was clear - and ran.

At the local youth club one of our pals paid our entrance fee and soon we were down stairs in the cavern type dance floor doing the boogie with the rest of the crowd.

We invited two girls up for a dance, pretending within ourselves that we hadn't a care in the world. Inside, though, we were shaking with a mixture of excitement and fear.

Our hearts skipped a few beats when a girlfriend of mine ran over to me and burst out the news that the police were upstairs looking for us. In panic we ran to the back of the hall and kicked open the fire door. A high wall confronted us but we leapt it like stags and ran off into the darkness.

TO THE TRAINS

The railway station wasn't too far away and quickly we formed a plan to jump a train and head south to England. However, since it was now the early hours of the morning, we realised that we'd have to bunk up in one of the carriages till the trains began to run in the morning.

We realised also that the police weren't fools. They'd include the railway station in their search list. So, instead of going straight into an empty carriage, we lay on the embankment above the railway to observe what would happen.

Sure enough it wasn't long till the police arrived and started going through the empty carriages. At this point we both realised that the chances of getting out of town were just about zero. Having come to this realisation we decided to do the next best thing - as we saw it - and have a bit of fun with the police.

There were lumps of coal scattered about the ground where we lay. We picked up a handful each and began pelting them at the policemen.

Most of them rattled off the carriage roofs and windows but a few of them found their mark and brought cries of anger from the peelers and shouts of delight from us.

SURRENDER

Escaping again we roamed the streets till about four in the morning, on the way stealing milk and bread rolls from a baker's van. We knew, however, that it would only be a matter of time till the police caught up with us, so as this truth gradually sunk in we decided to go back to the police station and give ourselves up. This would make it easier for us at our court appearance next morning, we thought.

It was a great plan - or so we thought. However, it was to be badly thwarted. Just as we were about to step through the doors of the police station two big peelers pounced on us and dragged us inside. The fugitives had been caught!

Instead of us getting the credibility for having voluntarily given ourselves up, we suffered the ignominy of being re-arrested.

The police took no chances with us as they locked us away for a second time. We were each consigned to an individual cell with every bolt and bar in place - and the food hatches securely locked. There would be no escaping again.

MUM'S THE WORD

All the next morning we waited to be questioned about the break out but not a word was said. Even when we finally came before the court it wasn't mentioned. All the other charges were read out, the evidence heard and the sentences passed - but not a word was spoken about our escapade the previous evening.

In hindsight, I suppose the police kept quiet about it out of sheer embarrassment. There would have been a lot of questions to be asked and answered if the police had had to admit that two young fourteen year old miscreants had led the local officers of the law a merry dance all over Dumfries in the wee small hours of the morning.

The outcome of the court appearance was that we were both remanded in custody on the house-breaking charges. My dad was there and, to give credit where credit is due, he spoke up for me. In fact, he offered a large sum of money to have me released on bail, but the court would hear none of it. We were to be sent to a remand home in Ayr for fourteen days. On top of that, the court wanted reports on our backgrounds.

SCHOOL FOR SCOUNDRELS

The remand home, like many other similar detention centres, was one big school for crime. I suppose that shouldn't come as a shock when you remember that the place played host to all the worst examples of young manhood from a large part of southern Scotland - and all under one roof.

The young lads there did their best to out- brag one another with their daring feats of crime. Dandy and I told of our escape. I dramatised the events taking care not to overdo it but creating enough of an impression to make sure that we wouldn't be picked on by the older, harder boys They all seemed suitably impressed.

The two weeks in Ayr passed fairly uneventfully and at the end of them we were brought back to Dumfries for another court appearance. After hearing the police and social services reports on us, the judge didn't take long to assess the situation and hand each of us a two- year probation sentence. Looking over the top of his glasses and furrowing his brow to make himself look even more stern, he delivered us a lecture on the seriousness of what we had done. With a strong exhortation to us to buck up our outlook on life, he dismisssed us from his presence. Sadly, his wise words washed over us.

Chapter Seven

LEADER OF THE PACK

I was now approaching my fifteenth birthday. Soon I'd be saying good-bye, for the last time, to school. My educational record was appalling, so my prospects for employment were anything but good. Added to this I two convictions for underage drinking, one from the sheriff court, one from a juvenile court. And then, there was that fortnight spent in the remand home at Ayr. Not a very good C.V. for a lad looking for work.

My main weakness was the drink which was beginning to play a bigger and bigger part in the problems which beset me. Before I left school I was putting away at least three half bottles of wine every week. And that wasn't all. There were cans and bottles of beer as well.

Sadly, my dad wasn't any help to me. On the contrary, he was a definite hindrance. Once, when I came home for lunch, my dad was sitting there in his chair drinking. He was, as we say "well on." After making me promise not to tell mum what we were up to he allowed me a mixture of wine and limeade to drink. After a few of these, not surprisingly, I was drunk and falling out with my dad.

GANG MASTER

By this time I was leading a pack of over twenty young people - twelve boys and about eight or ten girls. My leadership was maintained by a continuously violent attitude to everyone else in the gang. However, every now and then leadership has to be tested. Sometimes these tests were a bit dangerous - even foolhardy.

One night one of the gang members, a lad called Camel, produced a bottle of tablets and claimed they were his dad's pep pills. To prove myself the big man, I took the bottle from him and downed six of them at one go. I would show them I was their worthy leader. What a shock I was in for.

Nothing happened for about ten minutes. Then - bam! They hit me. I started acting in the most weird fashion. First there was the aggression - to everything and everyone about me. Then I began to hallucinate in the most weird way.

THE HUMAN ORANGE

Unbelievably, I took more of the tablets. The hallucination increased. I was now completely out of my mind. At one stage I rolled on the floor calling out to those around me "Don't peel me! I'm a human orange!"

The bursts of anger returned. My friends appeared to me as strange and frightening shadows, indistinct and unrecognisable - so I attacked them.

They decided, wisely, that I should be taken home. Bundling me into his car one of the club leaders drove me home. How he kept me in the car and how I behaved on the journey I don't know. Somehow, however, we arrived at my house safely.

My dad was there, with my brother, who had come up from the south for a few days to visit us. They were both drinking. His only response was to pack me upstairs to bed to sleep off the effects of the drugs.

MUSIC

I did sleep for a while but then was awakened by the sound of loud music. It's funny how music always seems louder upstairs than in the room where it's being played. However, I staggered downstairs to investigate and just as I pulled open the living room door my dad came walking out. For no reason whatever I punched him full in the face with such force that he was knocked to the ground.

Staggering on into the living room I was confronted by my brother. He stood up to remonstrate with me and I grabbed him by the lapels of his jacket, intending to floor him as I had floored my dad. Unlike my dad, however, he was prepared for my attack and using his superior strength threw me to the floor instead. He shouted at me, asking what was the matter. But I heard nothing - or if I did it didn't register - I was too far gone. Such was the power of these drugs.

Picking myself up I staggered from the living room into the kitchen and drove my fist straight through the window pane, cutting my arm in the process. My brother followed after me and, taking advantage of the fact that this incident had somewhat disorientated me, grabbed me again. He threw me to the ground and began to punch me, calling on my dad, who had now recovered from my initial punch, to assist him. They pinned me to the ground and rained blow after blow on my face.

HOSPITAL

They must have knocked me unconscious because the next memory I have is of wakening up next morning in the local mental hospital. What a situation! Just out of school a few weeks and here I was in the local lunatic asylum. "Where next?" I thought.

A nurse appeared and sought to console me. "Don't worry," she said. "You've taken an overdose of tablets and we're just keeping you here till we find out what those tablets were and what effect they've had on you."

FACE LIKE A PLUMB

I felt the need to go to the toilet and made my way there by myself. My face was aching so when I got to the toilet I took a look at myself in the mirror. The sight that looked back at me almost gave me a heart attack. Through the tiny slits of my eyes I could see what looked for all the world like a large blue plumb.

As I say, my eyes were mere slits. My lips and ears were three times their normal size and my nose had been flattened. My brother and my dad had certainly given me a pounding.

In the hospital there were long sessions with the psychiatric doctors. They asked about my home life, school-days, likes and dislikes, hobbies, friends, in fact, just about everything you can think of. I don't think they made much of me, however. I wonder what their reports said.

Back home my dad was still sporting a black eye - the consequence of the punch I had given him. When I saw him I was really sorry. I loved my dad, although we weren't that close to one another, and he didn't really deserve a black eye. However, both my parents forgave me once more and, for a while, all was quiet again.

THE HARD MAN

Coming up to my sixteenth birthday I was developing the "hard man" image more and more. The books I read, the films I went to see were all chosen with the object of helping me to model myself on the characters portrayed. With my dad having a second hand shop I had easy access to paperbacks.

In one of these books the main character cut and slashed his way through Glasgow's street life. In another the central figure was again a street fighter. These fantasy characters inspired me to this same kind of tough life style. I wanted to be the living embodiment of them. It seemed I was well on my way.

GRETNA GREEN

Just before my sixteenth birthday I decided to get the gang together for a really special night. On a Friday evening we all herded on to the bus and headed for Gretna. There was a place there called Gretna Dancing and it was a big attraction for young people.

Since about seven o'clock that night I had been drinking and we had a stock of booze with us on the bus. So by the time we arrived in Gretna I was well charged up and ready for anything.

The leader of the Gretna gang was a guy called Pedro. Shortly after we arrived our eyes clashed across the dance floor. It looked like there was going to be trouble. If there was, I was ready for it. Indeed, I could hardly wait for it. My opportunity came sooner than I expected.

One of the guys from our gang was dancing with a girl from Gretna. Without provocation Pedro walked over to them and stuck his head in the fella's face, splitting his nose. As soon as I saw the blood pouring down my mate's face I was over there for revenge. However, the bouncers were in first and escorted Pedro out of the dance hall. His gang trouped out behind him.

FIGHT!

Signalling to my boys, we followed. From the top of the stairway I caught sight of Pedro and his gang at the bottom. We stared daggers at each other.

"How about a battle in the car park?" I offered. "Yea, how about you and me face to face to the finish?" was his reply. "And whoever wins between you and me will rule the dancing," he added.

Such an open challenge, in front of the rest of my gang, couldn't be ignored. Even though Pedro was older and bigger than me and had something of a reputation for leaving his victims in a mess, I had to fight him.

In the car park all our mates formed a long line. I suppose each wanted to be in the front row for this big showdown. As soon as I had taken off my jacket, Pedro lunged wildly at me catching my thigh with his boot. He followed this with a punch which slammed into my forehead and left me sprawled on the ground.

WHAT A SCRAP!

The assembled crowd of lads from both gangs erupted in yells and boos at such a dramatic start to the scrap. Both sides were baying for blood. Before the night was out they would see plenty.

Pedro landed another boot into my ribs, then dropped on me with his full weight, driving the breath from my lungs. Maintaining his advantage, he pinned my arms to the ground with his knees and pounded his fists into my ribs time after time.

As I lay there below him and at his mercy, I was astonished at his power and speed. Above me was a wild, writhing, creature - his flailing arms and long, streaming locks of hair giving him an animal-like appearance. It was the long hair that gave me an idea for turning the tables.

In my hip pocket I carried a steel comb, sharpened like a knife. Drawing in one great breath, I heaved him up and managed to free my pinioned arms. Reaching for the comb with one hand, I grabbed his hair with the other and pulled him back towards me with a violent tug.

MOB TACTICS

Our faces were pressed so tightly together that he didn't see me raise the comb towards his left ear. I dug it in like a chisel and dragged it down the side of his face opening a gash that spurted blood like a fountain. Pedro emitted a loud scream as the pain ripped through him. He fell backwards screaming in agony.

Now I was on the offensive. Showing him as little mercy as he had shown me, I jumped on him. The fingers of my right hand found the inside of his gaping mouth and seized a handful of flesh. As he fought to get free I held on grimly and pulled. My grip was vise-like and soon the skin at one corner of his mouth began to tear.

Pedro was now screaming like a stuck pig. Helpless to defend himself and powerless to fight back, he begged for mercy. I showed him none. Standing up, I grabbed him by the now blood soaked locks of hair and dragged him backwards to where the members of his gang stood crestfallen and dumbfounded. Now, in a final defiant show of bravado, I picked him up and ran him headlong into their midst. The screams of delight from the boys in my gang was better music than I had heard all night.

TRIUMPH!

What a triumphant ride we had back home to Dumfries! We recounted the fight blow by blow and scoffed at the way Pedro had screamed and begged for mercy. I was a hero to the boys in my gang, admired and loved even more by the girls. Power and strength seemed to pulse through my body. This violent way of life excited and thrilled me. It was like a drug and I wanted more.

Chapter Eight

GANG WARFARE

The hard man image appealed to me. More and more I looked upon myself as a tough nut, someone not to be messed with. Every chance to prove the point was jumped at.

Once, after spending an evening with my girlfriend and a mate, drinking and listening to soul music, I was walking my girlfriend home.

Anne and I were walking hand in hand across the Troqueer bridge on the way to her house. The wine and beer had made us quite merry and we were both in a good mood, laughing and joking. Life was good.

Across the road five men, strangers to me, began shouting at us. Their remarks were rude and uncomplimentary and in a second my dander was up. Telling Anne to stay put I strolled across to where they stood and asked them, with a few oaths and curses for good measure, just who they thought they were talking to.

Without another word being spoken one of them stepped forward to attack me. He had hardly taken the first step when I booted him in the groin and he slumped to the pavement groaning with pain.

The biggest of the group took a bottle from a carrier bag and came at me with fury in his eyes. I gave him the same treatment as I had given the first one, sending the bag flying, smashing its contents against the wall.

BAGPIPE

Stepping over my second victim I grabbed a piece of broken glass from the bag and prepared to face the next of them. Just as I swung around a guy I knew as Bagpipe took a swing at me. He missed and as the momentum of his lunge took him past me, I stuck the piece of broken bottle into his throat. He, too, fell to the ground, crying in pain, clutching his throat and trying to stanch the torrent of blood that flowed from the open wound.

Three down, two to go. Would I be able to deal with the others? The answer came swiftly as a bottle crashed down on my head and the lights went out.

The wail of police sirens and the flashing of ambulance lights was the next thing I knew. In the hospital casualty department they inserted a few stitches in my head wound and then the police wanted to see me. They took a statement, let me go and I breathed a sigh of relief. However, my five assailants were each charged with assault and breach of the peace.

SEEDTIME AND HARVEST

At home mum and dad still had the odd row, especially when drink was taken, but on the whole, life there had settled down a good bit. They were both concerned about the lifestyle I had chosen and I suppose wondered where it was going to lead. However, when you think about it, it was a bit late in the day for them to be anxious about me. They had sown the seeds of my wildness by the example they had set for years. Those seeds were now beginning to produce their own frightful harvest.

At about this time few of my mates and myself formed a new gang. We called it "The Border." The gang had about a dozen young men who were really committed to it and lots of other boys and girls who followed us.

Every week-end we were involved in some sort of trouble. The local dances were usually the scene of pitched battles between our gang and the locals in whatever area we chose to visit. Once, at Lockerbie, there was such a riot involving our gang and a bus load of Rangers football supporters that it took about twenty police officers from several local districts to bring it under control. There were stabbings, heads cracked open with beer bottles, people beaten up and many left unconscious.

CHRISTMAS FUN

On Christmas Eve 1967 my mum and dad and myself were returning home from the local King's Arms Hotel when we met a friend of mine called Blacky. He took me aside and asked if I'd like to go with him down to Carlisle. "I've got a car," he said. Then dropping his voice to a whisper he added "I've got a couple of bottles of wine too. There's a party in Carlisle. It'll be great. Plenty of birds too."

My parents had to be convinced but that didn't take too long. I could be a pretty charming and persuasive character when I needed to be. Assured that I was getting a lift there and back they agreed. So, with a big hug for my mum and a "Thank you," to my dad we were off.

"Right," said Blacky "I've got the keys to the gas board's van - the one I use for work every day. It'll do us nicely."

Even though Blacky worked for the gas board I was pretty sure he wouldn't be allowed to use the van outside working hours, so I asked him point blank "Is it O.K. if we take it?"

Instead of answering my question Blacky cracked open one of the bottles of wine, took a few gulps from it and handed it to me. After a few slurps, I too soon forgot the question.

In a couple of minutes we were at the gates of the gas board's yard. Blacky opened the gate, headed for the garage and in a few minutes we were roaring down the road towards Carlisle. The second bottle of wine was broken open and as we passed it back and forth between us our sense of mirth and freedom increased.

We had only gone a few miles when we became aware of bright lights following us. On closer scrutiny it turned out to be one of those big white traffic patrol cars. Whether or not the police were suspicious of us at this point I'll never know, but they were certainly tailing us.

ROAD RAGE

Perhaps if we hadn't been drinking we might have done the sensible thing and driven carefully and at the proper speed. But we had been drinking and the drink was having an effect. We raced on wildly.

The siren wailed, the lights flashed and we were signalled to stop. As far as I was concerned, we were not for stopping. I shouted to Blacky to put his foot down and get away from them. Well, he tried it but without much success. The gas board's van wasn't built for speed. Come to think of it, it wasn't built for comfort either. Flat out, it did about sixty miles an hour - hardly the machine for a high speed chase.

We did get away from them for a bit but it was only a matter of time till they were on our tail again, lights still flashing, siren still wailing. Blacky kept his foot pressed hard to the floor, weaving and swerving to prevent the police car from overtaking. As it happened, they never did get past - they didn't need to.

With the van's engine screaming for mercy, Blacky kept his foot hard down and pointed the van into the next bend at top speed. As I've said, the van wasn't built for great speed, but it wasn't designed for cornering at anything more than a moderate pace either. Halfway round the bend a wall suddenly appeared and we headed straight for it.

"We've had it!" cried Blacky and then, after what seemed an age the van slammed into the wall. The crunching, scraping, smashing sounds were deafening but they were nothing to the terror we felt as the van tumbled over and over like a tin box, throwing us about inside like a couple of toy dolls. Then, blackness!

CASUALTY

Consciousness returned very, very slowly. As it did, I was aware of great pain in almost every part of my body. It was pain such as I'd never experienced before. We must have been rattled around inside that van even more than I'd imagined. I felt like I'd been kicked from Land's End to John O'Groats.

As I became more and more aware of my surroundings it became clear that, once again, I was back in hospital. My groanings alerted a young nurse who came rushing to my bedside to reassure me.

"You're all right," she whispered. "You're going to be fine. You've hurt your back and we don't want you moving about too much, not for a day or two."

ANGELS

Her words came like a soothing balm to my troubled spirit. Here was someone well practised in the art of comfort. What a blessed group of individuals these angels of mercy are. No words can ever praise them enough, no money can ever pay them enough for the healing ministry they provide.

The nurse's presence seemed to dispel the pain. When she left it came flooding back again. They had laid me on a bed of boards with no pillow. It was Christmas Day but instead of me enjoying the message of "peace on earth and goodwill toward men," I was languishing in the most excruciating pain I'd ever known.

Two other men in that ward did nothing to ease my suffering. Every breath I drew seemed to aggravate the pain. I groaned in agony and my groanings upset my fellow patients opposite. They called to me to "give over," to "shut up," to "give their heads peace!" It turned out they were policemen who had come out the wrong side of a hit-and-run incident. No wonder they had little sympathy for a young crook like me. I was the victim of my own stupidity - they were victims of someone else's.

CRIPPLED

Three days after the accident the doctors came to tell me the result of my injuries. As well as the obvious facial abrasions and other bruising, there was concussion, cracked ribs and a fractured vertebra in my spine. This was the most serious of all. The others would heal with time. The fractures would affect me for the rest of my life.

The consequence of this cracked vertebra was that the nerves which controlled my feet had been deadened. The effect was that I no longer had control of my feet. They both dropped forward and hung limp. Try as I might I couldn't flex my ankles. How would I walk?

"Why me?" was my immediate reaction to the news of my most serious injury. I suppose I should really have been asking "Why not me?" However, when you're heart is devoid of the grace of God and you've lived a life that is self seeking and wicked, you don't think the way you ought to. Wallowing in self-sympathy was the natural human reaction.

Blacky, the guy who had inveigled me into this mess, had come off much better than I had done. He had a black eye, a few bruises and would have to face his bosses at the gas board. But that was it. He was released from hospital after a day.

BETTER DEAD

"It would have been better for me if I had died," I thought. "How am I going to live if I can't walk? What does the world want with a cripple?" Deep depression settled down over my soul like a great, dark blanket.

In Edinburgh they had much better expertise and more up-to-date equipment. I was to be taken there the next day for a more thorough examination. In the mean time my mum and dad arrived to see me. They were very kind - and sympathetic - and they told me not to worry.

"Everything will be fine," they said. "We'll see you through this." The guilt I felt, as they sat there comforting me, only made my bitterness worse.

My mum went with me in the ambulance to Edinburgh. As we rode along I couldn't help feeling sorry for her. All her life she had known little else than misery and sorrow. Here she was again having to deal with a situation which wasn't of her making.

My mother was a good woman at heart. Most of the misery she suffered was thrust upon her through the cruelty and selfishness of my father. He drunk to excess. That, literally, drove my mother to drink and then, in the heat of the moment, she said things that she didn't really mean. No wonder there were so many rows in our house! But now, watching her as we rode in the ambulance, I seemed to detect a new look about her. She seemed more at ease; almost relieved that I would be out of commission for a while. Maybe now she would get a chance to mother me properly.

Chapter Nine

You'll Never Walk Again

A t Edinburgh's Royal Hospital, I was taken immediately to Ward 20. Ward 20 dealt with accidents and emergencies. I had been put on, or is it into, a "Striker Frame." That's a special bed for people with spinal injuries. The striker frame is just wide enough for one body and holds the patient in a fairly constricted position. This is deliberate, since movement can make spinal injuries worse, especially in the first few days after an accident.

This bed was to become my home for the next four months. Every two hours, a nurse came and screwed the top half of the bed to the lower half, on which I was lying. With me between the two halves, like the meat in a sandwich, the whole frame was turned through 180 degrees. Now, instead of me lying on my back, I was lying face down. In another two hours the turning operation was reversed. I was lying face up again.

My poor mother left the hospital that day in a rather tearful state. She did her best to console me, assuring me that it wouldn't be long till I was home again. It had been a long time since I had seen such strength in her.

WARD 20

Ward 20 was a pretty grim place. The day after I arrived, another striker bed was wheeled in and parked right beside mine. On it lay a miner, who had broken his neck in a pit accident. Two metal pins had been placed in his neck and he was suspended in such a way as to make movement of the head impossible.

Across the way there was Bruce, who had been hit by a bus and knocked off his scooter. His whole head was shaved, revealing a great scar which ran from his forehead to the back of his neck.

Then there was Lindsay, brain damaged as a result of another traffic accident; and little Sarah who was only four years old. She stood in her cot all day long, whistling through a tracheotomy fitting in her throat, every time she breathed.

Davy was the victim of another mining tragedy. A blast had caught him full in the face, destroying the whole bone structure and leaving him looking like something from a horror movie. Sadly, he was also totally paralysed.

HORRORS EVERY DAY

Every day brought some new victim of disaster. One in particular stands out above the others. The quietness of an early morning was suddenly shattered by an ear-splitting scream. It came from the bed of the lorry driver who had been brought in during the night. As the anaesthetic wore off, he became aware of his whereabouts and situation. Looking down, he discovered that both his legs had been amputated and this, understandably, was what prompted the scream and then the yells.

When my parents arrived on the following Sunday, the doctors asked to speak to them privately. When they came back to my bedside, all three had the gravest of looks on their faces. Quite matter of factly, the doctor explained to me that I would never walk again. He was very sorry to bring such news to one so young but in his opinion, the diagnosis was accurate and final. My mother and father were advised that our house would have to be renovated to accommodate a wheel-chair.

It wasn't till later that night that the full impact of this news sunk in. "Sixteen years old, " I thought "and now, a cripple." What would my mates think of me? In the past I had laughed at people with disabilities. I had mocked their misfortune. Now, I was joining their ranks. Strangely, a verse from the Bible came to my mind and hit me with terrifying force.

"Whatsoever a man soweth, that shall he also reap."   However, this only made me more stubborn. "I'll show them who's not going to walk," I murmured.

Eventually the long haul on the striker bed came to an end. A week before I was due to be allowed to lie in a real bed, I was moved to a convalescent home in another part of Edinburgh.

The first day there wonderful - well, nearly wonderful. There was a whole different atmosphere about this place. It was much more relaxed and really friendly and it did a lot for my emotional stability as well. I didn't feel nearly so twisted up inside.

A BIG EVENT

For the first time in nineteen weeks I was to be allowed out of bed. What an event this would be! The nurses gathered around and a wheel-chair was brought up close to my bed. A plastic jacket, like the top half of a medieval suit of armour, was strapped around my chest. This was to keep my upper body absolutely rigid and prevent any possibility of further spinal damage. I couldn't bend over. I couldn't twist. I was like a waxwork model.

Two of the nurses took an arm each and very slowly and gently lifted me up. Then, carefully they moved me to the edge of the bed and prepared to lower me into the wheel-chair. Everything was going well till my feet touched the floor. It seemed like there must have been a sudden slight jolt or something because the next thing I was aware of was a technicolor display of stars and stripes. You know the kind of thing you see in the comic books when Desperate Dan biffs the baddie.   Then blackout!

When I awoke there was a nurse by my side. She explained that it was perfectly normal for patients to faint after spending such a long time lying prone. I suppose it's something to do with the blood rushing from the head. Anyway, the good thing about all this was that I was now lying in luxurious comfort. I had said good-bye to the striker.

Next day they were successful in getting me into the wheel-chair - and no fainting this time. After a week I was an expert at manoeuvring this new mode of transport and felt a great new sense of freedom.

THE FUNNY SIDE

It's amazing how, even in the midst of tragedy, humour, or at least a sense of fun, can creep into daily events. Bob was another wheel-chair patient. He and I became quite friendly and one day he asked me about my injuries. "Dropped feet," I explained. "Oh!" he said. "That's my problem too, only mine have dropped right off." At this he lifted up the blanket covering his knees to reveal the stumps where his legs used to be. Then he told me his story.

"I'm a publican, John. One day I was helping to unload a beer lorry when one of the kegs slipped and fell on my feet. My injuries developed into gangrene, so there was nothing else they could do but take them off!"

A physiotherapist worked with me at the convalescent centre every day. She was very good - and very encouraging. I'd only been there a few days when she told that she'd seen other patients walk again after being given a diagnosis similar to mine. Since I was so young she thought there was a very good chance I would walk again. I want to thank that young woman today. She gave me one of the greatest gifts ever - the hope to go on.

Next day I was measured for leg callipers. Ten days later the unusual contraptions, plus two elbow crutches, arrived. When I stood up, with the callipers, the crutches and the aforementioned breastplate, I resembled something out of Robocop. My first movements went a long way towards completing the image.

TIN LEGS

Just like in the film "Reach for the Sky," when wartime flying ace, Douglas Bader, first got his "tin legs," as he called them, the physio stood about fifteen yards in front of me and beckoned me to walk. Two nurses held me on either side and I took my first tiny, shuffling step in three months. I made it all the way to the physio as well.

Everyone, except me, was delighted with this first attempt at walking again. Human nature being what it is, I wanted to do better. I wanted to throw away the crutches, get rid of the callipers and jump and skip all the way home to Dumfries. However, realistically, that would take a while.

I kept practising with the callipers and crutches, but it was difficult. Progress was slow. They made a clanking noise as I walked and they looked awful. I was embarrassed using them - but then what option did I have?

NEW TECHNOLOGY

Not long after this a Professor Alfred came to see me. He was from the Royal Hospital in Edinburgh and he said he had some news for me. Some new fitments for people with my types of injuries had been invented in West Germany and he wanted to know if I'd like to try them out - be a sort of guinea-pig. He went on the explain that these new contraptions were made of plastic and shaped like booties. They fitted over the foot and the ankle and had a large hole cut in the front of them to allow the toes to peep through. Over the top of these I wore my ordinary shoes or boots.

"Do you mean to say that when you wear these new booties you can't see any callipers?" I asked. "There are no callipers," he said. "These take the place of callipers."

"Lead me to them," I thought, but replied politely "I don't mind trying them."

Almost immediately plaster casts of my feet were made. These were used as moulds to make the booties and in a few weeks they arrived. I couldn't wait to try them out.

Professor Alfred and his team huddled round me while the new walking aids were fitted to my feet. Then came the moment of truth. I stood up - and with the aid of only one walking stick set off down the ward. I could walk all right but the pain was excruciating, However, lest they felt tempted to abandon the experiment, I pretended they were fine and kept on walking. At the same time I was prepared for almost any pain so long as I could be rid of those awful looking callipers.

HOME

By the beginning of July the doctors told me that I was fit enough to go home. I phoned my parents immediately and, as well as expressing their delight, they promised to arrange transport home to Dumfries.

Most of that last day in the hospital was spent with my friend Bob who had a locker full of booze. Almost every day for the last three months we had met in his room and downed a few cans of beer together.

Bob had been like a substitute father to me, encouraging me and comforting me. Having lived a longer and fuller life, he had the benefit of experience and was able to pass on many a wise word.

As I left the hospital the next day my only tinge of regret was in saying good-bye to Bob. I looked at him, sitting there alone in his wheelchair, with not much hope of improvement, and I felt so sorry for him.

My dad had been banned for driving whilst drunk, so my brother Jim, my friend Gus and their wives came to collect me. They all said how well I looked, helped to bundle me into the car and off we sped to Dumfries.

God commendeth His love toward us, in that,
while we were yet sinners, Christ died for us.

Romans 5:8

Chapter Ten

BACK TO THE WILD LIFE

Now you'd think that, after all I'd been through, I would have learned a bit of sense. Sadly, the heart of man being what it is, and mine having undergone no change, I was just as much a prey to foolishness and sin as I'd ever been.

My attitude was "I have Christmas, New Year and my birthday to make up for, so - let's get straight back into the drink." After all I had proved the doctors wrong. I had walked again. Why shouldn't I celebrate with a few wee bevvys.

At home, nothing else had changed. Mum and dad were still hitting the bottle quite hard. And there were still the battles afterwards. "Another good reason for me to drink myself stupid now and again," I reasoned.

THE MENACE

There were changes to the gang as well. Since I had been knocked out of commission, another lad had taken my place. He was popularly referred to as "The Menace" and was older, stronger and fitter than I. The rest of the gang, who had been so loyal to me, fell in behind his leadership. Naturally, I was squeezed out.

All that I'd been through, plus the injuries, the difficulty in walking and the fact that my place at the head of the gang had been taken by another, brought the dark clouds of depression down upon my spirit. I was also still in great pain. My cure was drink, as much as I could get. Of course, the more I drunk the more I wanted.

Two weeks after my release from hospital the police arrived at my door with summonses in connection with the theft of the gas board's van. "Had I not suffered enough," I thought. "After all I didn't steal the van. I was only the passenger. It wasn't even my idea!"

However, in the eyes of the law, I was an accessory to the crime and deserved to be punished. Punished I was. A £40 fine and banned from driving for thirteen years. I couldn't figure out how a lad who had never been behind the wheel of a car could be banned for thirteen years. But there you are.

This further brush with the law did nothing to improve my relationships with the police. I hated them even more and determined to continue on my own way.

GEORDIE AND PEEM

About a week later I sat, alone, in a pub in town. At my side, in a plastic bag, there was about a third of a bottle of vodka. Over at the bar some of my old mates stood drinking and laughing. "Were they laughing at me?" I wondered. Propped against the chair beside me was my walking stick. How I hated it. If only I was the fit young lad I used to be.

Over at the Juke Box, Geordie, a wee hard man, was acting the fool. When he caught sight of me he came over and sat down beside me. "You're Peem," he said. Peem was my old nick-name.

"How about getting me a drink?" he asked in a demanding kind of way. "Get your own drink!" I snapped back. Taken aback by this insolence from someone who obviously was in no position to take it any farther, he directed his next remark to the boys at the bar. "Listen to this tin bum," he laughed "listen to the cripple! Who does he think he is?"

I was seething inside, wishing I could stand up and give him a bit of the treatment I'd dished out to so many people in the past. Somehow, however, I managed to control my feelings and button my lip.

Because of the racket coming from the Juke Box most of the boys at the bar had heard none of this conversation. Those who had picked up a few words ignored them. They were just as drunk as Geordie.

A MALICIOUS INVITATION

"Listen Geordie," I said, in a conspiratorial voice - just loud enough to be heard above the music. "Listen Geordie. I've a bottle of vodka here. If we slip into the toilet I'll share it with you." Geordie's eyes lit up with delight. "Great!" he said, and followed me towards the gents.

I swung the toilet door open and beckoned Geordie to step inside. As the door swung closed behind me I could see there was nobody else about.

Geordie swung round to face me and as he did so I lifted the bottle from the bag. "I was only joking when I made that wee remark about the cripple," Geordie apologised.

"That's O.K. Geordie," I responded softly. "We all say things we don't mean sometimes. Just forget it." Intending to help him forget it I brought the bottle down on his head with all my might. As the fragments of glass scattered to the four walls Geordie slumped silently to the floor. Not a sound crossed his lips.

I stood above him, the jagged neck of the bottle still in my hand. Blood poured from the open wound across his forehead and ran down into his eyes. Recovering himself a little he grabbed for the handle of the toilet door with one hand and took hold of the end of my walking stick with the other. As he struggled I hit him again, full force, across the face and left him lying almost unconscious. Slowly and calmly I walked out into the cool night air, my only regret the loss of the vodka.

PROGRESS

When I left the hospital, arrangements were made for me to go back every so often for check- ups on my progress and consultations with the physiotherapist. These, however, were eventually abandoned. Late night drinking sprees left me with a hangover so often that I never turned up for the appointments. What was the purpose of arranging any more? What's more, I had learned over the period of time to walk without the aid of a stick. So I was making progress.

Despite my conflict with society, there was within me a desire to do better; a feeling that it was time I pulled myself together. In an effort to put this into practice I took up an offer of a job.

One of my dad's friends was a chef and he very kindly fixed me up with a position as a trainee. The job was in a hotel about twenty miles from home. In due course, I arrived for work and discovered, to my pleasant surprise, that the hotel was situated in an old castle. It had a beautiful setting, in lovely grounds, with plenty of open space and lots of trees. "This oasis, away from the jungle of the big town, would be good for me," I thought.

Stepping in through the large stone portals into the entrance hall, I was met by one of the bosses who explained the hours I would have to work, the wage I'd be paid and what my duties would consist of. A gentleman then was detailed to show me to my room. It turned out to be at the very top of one of the towers of the castle.

As I climbed the spiral staircase, floor after floor, to the top of the house I fought a constant battle against the pain in my feet. With a suitcase in one hand and no stick to help me it was difficult to disguise my unsteadiness, but I managed.

UNPACKING

The porter left me alone in this little round room and, throwing my case on the bed, I sprang the locks and began to unpack. When the last pair of socks was chucked into a drawer I closed it and walked over to the window to consider the view. Standing there, dreamily gazing across the beautiful landscape, I pondered my good fortune.

Here I was, a young lad from the wrong side of the tracks, getting a fresh, new start - a chance to prove himself. This was also the first time I'd be responsible for looking after myself. I hoped I'd face up to both challenges successfully.

However, at the end of this brief reverie I walked back over to the suitcase which still lay open on the bed. An cut-throat razor was the only item I hadn't unpacked. I lifted it now, walked back over to the window and hid it down the back of one of the shutters. Perhaps you think it sad that I still needed something from the outside world to give me a sense of security, but in those days, that's the way my mind worked.

LIFE IN THE KITCHEN

The first week's work in the kitchen went very well. I spent the days washing and preparing vegetables for the chef. I diced carrots, sliced onions, dressed fish, kept the stock-pot fresh and changed the oil in the deep fat fryers. Helping me with this work was another lad from Glasgow. John was about thirty-five, a hard worker and a hard drinker too.

Every day, after lunch, we had a three hour break before we began work on the dinners. During these breaks there wasn't much to do except play cards. So, we played cards.

One day, during my second week at the job, the card school met in my room. After a while the kitty had built up nicely, there was booze on the table and smoke filled the air. We were having a great time. John, the guy from Glasgow, had lost most of his money to the under-manager. Naturally, this made him somewhat uneasy.

CHEATING

It was my turn to deal again. As I shuffled the pack and threw the cards in front of the players John suddenly turned nasty. He felt he was being cheated out of his money and he accused me and the under-manager of being in league to do it. Half drunk, he lifted a beer bottle as if to throw it at me. The fourth member of our card school, another kitchen porter, grabbed his arm and took the bottle. I screamed back at John "I'm no cheat! Can't you take your beating like a man?"

John let fly with a punch and caught me on the side of the head. Stunned by the blow and reeling with pain I fell to one side and let out a stream of oaths and curses. The other two lads grabbed him and bundled him out of the room slamming the door behind them. John was still shouting at me, calling me a lying, cheating little swine and returning my oaths.

For the next five minutes, I lay on the bed seething with rage. My head was reeling, my ear was ringing with the pain and every moment the fury within me boiled hotter and hotter. A look in the mirror revealed only minor damage from the blow he had struck. A small cut bled slightly and was easily cleaned up with a dab from a damp cloth. However, it was enough to create a great new swell of anger within me. I must have revenge.

REVENGE

The razor was still tucked behind the window shutter. Now was the time to retrieve it. Slipping it into my back pocket I crept quietly down the stars and along the corridor to the kitchen. John was hunched over the deep-fat fryer making chips for his tea. The noise of bubbling fat and his preoccupation with what he was doing allowed me to creep up on him undetected.

Clutching the razor tightly in my hand I leapt forward screaming at him. Before he knew it I was on him and the razor was digging into his back just below the neck. I pulled it downwards and it dug in so deep that I could hear it scrape on the bone of his shoulder blade. As the razor dug into his flesh John emitted a long, low pitched whistle and grabbed the handle of the fish fryer basket more tightly to steady himself.

I brought the razor down into his back again feeling a great sense of satisfaction welling up within me. This time the cut was not so deep, but already his white coat was turning crimson as the blood gushed from his open wounds.

John collapsed to the floor in a heap but almost immediately sprang to his feet again. He was like a wild animal now, like a bull who had just been spiked and sought revenge. He ran blindly around the kitchen with me in hot pursuit, still intent on inflicting even more damage.

With another wild swing I caught him again, just above the waist. Once more the razor found its mark, penetrating his shirt and opening another long wound in his chest. In an effort to escape my wrath John fled the kitchen and ran out into the corridor with me in hot pursuit. I was getting my revenge and it was sweet, but still I wanted more.

PANIC!

At that the chef manager and other members of the hotel staff burst onto the scene. Astounded by the sight that met them, they attempted to separate us. The chef manager pleaded with me to leave John alone and tried to grab hold of me. In panic, I made for the back door of the kitchen and ran outside, down the gardens and into a thicket, where I hid.

I was so enraged that I was no longer in control of my actions. I still wanted to do damage to somebody or something. Incredibly, I pulled open my shirt and brought the razor across my stomach in one swift stroke. Immediately the blood appeared.

If I was caught the razor would be damning evidence so I hurled it from me. It buried itself in the undergrowth. A sharp piece of slate caught my eye and snatching it up I dug it into the wound, ripping it up and down several times. In hysterics I stood there blubbering and crying, not knowing what to do next. So, I ran! From the thicket I sprinted across the lawn and down to a pond, where I threw the slate into the water.

Spinning round I saw two policemen, just a few yards away, at the top of the bank overlooking the pond. Cautiously they approached me, at the same time blocking any chance of escape.

"It's all right John," they called out to me. "We don't want to harm you. We want to help you." At this point I collapsed.

I couldn't have been unconscious for long because when I opened my eyes again I was half way up the bank and being dragged along by the two policemen. The back doors of their Land Rover swung open and I was thrust inside.

PATCHED UP

The local hospital did a good job of patching me up but when I stepped out of the treatment room the police were waiting for me. They marched me down the long corridor, passing John, my victim, who was sitting on a bench, flanked on either side by two more officers.

When he saw me, he pulled the bath towel from around his naked shoulders and made a lunge for me. "Look what you've done to me you little coward!" he shouted.

There were three long, black railway tracks down his back. "Over a hundred stitches, you stinking little rat. "I suppose you think you're a real hard man." I tried to boot him again for his cheek but the policemen were too quick. One of them screwed my arm up my back and they both manoeuvred me out to the Land Rover.

Back at the police station they stuck me into a cell for a couple of hours to cool off. Afterwards, at the interview, the police issued me a stern warning and added "You must be the luckiest guy alive. The Glasgow joker doesn't want to prefer charges against you. Seems he has a record for violence and isn't long out of prison. But we know you did it. You should get ten years, and if we could find that razor you used you'll still be charged - by us."

DEATH WISH

Back in the cell I felt no remorse for what I had done. I did wonder, though, why I had turned on myself. It seemed as if I had some kind of a death wish. All evening I lay wondering what would happen to me. Would they search that thicket and find the knife? Would the cell door suddenly burst open and peelers come to take me away again? And if they did, what would be my fate? These perplexing thoughts raced through my troubled mind for hours till, at last, sleep dispelled them.

About seven o'clock next morning the key rattled in the lock, the cell door swung open and a policeman stood there. But the sudden panic which again gripped me was unfounded. The policeman simply walked me to the front office, gave me my belongings and informed me that no charges were being preferred.

The castle hotel was about four miles away so I asked the police if I could have a lift. "Walk!" was their terse reply. I walked.

CASE PACKED

Back at the hotel I made my way to the kitchen. The chef, quite matter of factly, said that my case was packed and that I would find it in the garage. Also, I could pick up my wages at reception. Nobody spoke to me. Even when the girl at the desk handed me an envelope containing my money and P45 form, not a word was said.

Walking down the avenue I turned and took a last look at the big castle hotel. I had arrived there with such hope, such determination. Alas, in just a few short days the dream was over. Once again I had fouled things up and I had no one to blame but myself.

Chapter Eleven

MAD PEEM!

At home in Dumfries the news of the fight in the hotel soon filtered through. It did me no harm amongst my peers. "Mad Peem," they called me now, and it was probably well justified. Every week brought some new incident which involved me; some new brush with the law. The death wish I referred to earlier almost seemed to be part of my internal make up. No where is this better exemplified than in what happened just a few weeks after I got back to Dumfries.

The drill hall was a great battle ground on a Friday night. Many a row broke out there, many a head was split, and many a person wished they'd never heard of the place.

On this particular Friday night I had drunk the entrance money, so couldn't pay my way in. However, this didn't mean abandoning the idea of gaining admittance. I would find a way in somehow.

Round the back of the drill hall, I found a drain pipe and started to climb it. I knew if I got onto the roof there was a sky-light which would let me drop into the gent's toilet.

In a half drunken state I began the ascent of the drain pipe. How I managed it with legs as bad as mine I don't know - but I did. Once on the roof I started to half walk, half crawl the short distance to the sky-light.

Suddenly my feet slipped from under me and I was sliding uncontrollably downwards. My feet hit the gutter and shot straight over. My knee caps were next to hit but they didn't stop me sliding inexorably on. As the rest of my body went over the edge I clawed with both hands hoping for a miracle. This wasn't to be a day for miracles.

SPLAT!

When my body hit the concrete, twenty-five feet below, there was a sound like wet clothes splatting into a sink. The force of the fall drove the breath from my lungs and left me semi-conscious.

The sound of running feet coming down the alley diverted my attention, momentarily, from my agony. Then they were all about me, a dozen voices all chattering at the same time. I heard oaths and curses of desperation; raised voices shouting instruction; excited screams from girls; calm instruction from the more sensible. Then slowly the familiar darkness gathered about me and I lost consciousness.

When I awoke I was back in hospital with the customary "angel of mercy" hovering over me. Despite falling over twenty-five feet on to solid concrete, I had sustained only a broken arm. The doctors said that my semi-drunken stupor had saved my life. My body and muscles were so relaxed that I had hit the ground just like a heavy weight boxer after a knock out punch.

MORE THUGGERY

Even with my broken arm in plaster I was still a force to be reckoned with. Once, while sitting with a friend in a cafe, he ventured a rather sarcastic remark. I let it pass at the time but had no intention of letting it pass altogether. Five minutes later, as we left the cafe and he was off guard, I swung the plastered arm round with all my might and caught him full on the face. Both his hands went up for protection and I booted him between the legs. Screaming in agony he doubled over and I hit him again, this time with my good fist, straight in the mouth. As I walked away I murmured to myself "That's the end of another good friendship!"

Just before my eighteenth birthday, another job offer came my way. It was in the catering trade again, this time as a "commis chef," in a hotel in King's Lynn, Norfolk. To get me out of the way of trouble in his home town, my dad financed the trip. At least this would put an end to the constant stream of policemen who came to our door looking for me.

ZORBA THE GREEK

Not far from the hotel where I worked there was a public house and, of course, I was a frequent customer there. It didn't take long to get into a fight either. A Greek guy, whom I quickly christened "Zorba," appointed himself spokesman for the rest of the pub crowd one night when I decided to render a few verses of "The Bonny, Bonny Banks of Loch Lomond."

It wasn't long till one side invited the other outside to settle matters, in the usual way, with fists. On this occasion, although I fought with all my former ferocity, Zorba came out the victor. I had the humiliation of having to surrender to a stronger man.

However, Zorba was magnanimous in victory, giving me a hearty handshake and saying to the onlookers "Don't be too hard on Jock, he's all right. If he hadn't been a bit drunk he'd have wiped me out." It turned out Zorba was the local hard man, reckoned to be the toughest guy in King's Lynn, so the fight established me as one of them and I joined their gang.

DRUGS

King's Lynn turned out to be another stepping stone on my downward path. It was there I was first introduced to hard drugs. I don't think it would be prudent to go into the lurid details of what drugs we tried, or the methods we used to take them. Suffice to say that every type of drug that was available was experimented with, and many of them we used again and again.

Drugs are dangerous, there's no getting away from that. It didn't take long for this style of living to have a dramatic and damaging effect on my body. I suffered rapid weight loss, ulcers in the mouth, continuous disorientation and, of course, many scrapes with the law.

We travelled all over the immediate countryside, to many towns, where drugs were available at dances and clubs. Sometimes we danced and popped drugs all night long.

SEANCE

Sometimes we got up to even more crazy stunts. One evening, at a party, we decided to have a seance. What happened next is a graphic illustration of the fearfulness of the powers of darkness.

The letters of the alphabet, the numbers one to ten and the words "Yes," and "No," were written on small pieces of paper and spread out on a table. A small glass was placed up-side-down in the centre of the table and we all sat around it in a circle. The lights were dimmed while two of the members of the group placed the tips of their fingers on the glass.

A few moments passed in silence, then, in a hushed voice, someone called out "Is there anyone there?"   After repeating the call several times the glass slowly began to move - and stopped at the word "YES."

Stunned for a moment we soon recovered our composure and courage enough to whisper the request   "Please spell out the message."

WARNING!

The glass began to move again. Slowly and steadily it spelled out "B.E.W.A.R.E. N.O.E.L."   We sat frozen in our seats as it came to a halt and waited to see if there was more. But it sat still.

"Do you mean Noel's in danger," was our next question. The glass was motionless.

"Please tell us if Noel's in any kind of trouble." All eyes were fixed on Noel who pretended to be unmoved by what had happened. Still, the glass remained stationery.

"Give us a sign if you're still there," we pleaded. The moments ticked on but there was no further message from the glass.

Suddenly the deathly silence of the room was shattered. With a terrifying shriek the cat leapt from its cosy seat by the fire and clung to the arm of one of the boys at the table. Panic stricken, he let out his own shriek of fear and jumped to his feet. The table was overturned, the pieces of paper and the glass scattered in all directions and everyone shouted and screamed in terror.

Then, the lights were on and we all stood in a frightened huddle. The lads tried to laugh it off as a big joke. Some of the girls began to cry. There's no doubt we were all moved by what had happened. Someone put on a record and gradually the music soothed us.

TRAGEDY

Noel and I had a quiet chat about the seance later and I asked him what he thought about the message of the glass. "Doesn't frighten me," he scoffed "it's all a bit of a laugh, isn't it?"

Two days later, as I sat in the local pub with my girlfriend, Penny, another girl came over to us with the news that Noel was dead. He was travelling home on his motor-scooter when he was involved in an accident. He died instantly.

All the members of the gang who had been at the seance were startled by the news of Noel's death, but nobody ever talked about it. They were probably too frightened. As for me, I never sat at a seance table again.

Chapter Twelve

DRINK AND DRUGS

After about six months in King's Lynn, the police began a serious crack down on the drug scene. News filtered through that they were looking for me so I thought it might be prudent to high-tail it back to Dumfries.

Drugs weren't so easy to come by at home so I resorted to the drink again, but in more abundant quantities. Drink always had a detrimental affect on my character. It turned me into a violent, hate ridden creature. The target for most of my hatred was the police. The very sight of a blue uniform drove me wild with antagonism.

Just before my twentieth birthday I was back in prison again. This time it was for my involvement in the smashing of Burton's shop window. I didn't do it, but I was along with the guy who did, so I got nabbed.

HAGGIS

In prison there were a few skirmishes too. I was the only Scots guy there and the others found it easy to pick on me. Nobody calls me a "stupid haggis" and gets away with it, was my philosophy. So, when another inmate did just that, I felled him with a metal tray.

Whilst in prison I wrote to my girlfriend regularly. We had decided to get married as soon as I was released, although how I ever imagined it would work is beyond me. I had no trade, no work, no means of income and so no way of supporting a wife. As well as that I was an incurable slave to drink. It was a crazy proposition.

Norma was a lovely lassie who had a good job as a typist at the factory where her father was foreman. I really did love her and we got on very well, except when I had drink taken. What she saw in a scoundrel like me I'll never know. As I say, we got on very well and I was never violent towards her, but she must have been upset many times by my dominant attitude and my selfish ways.

Norma often talked to me about her faith. She was a Roman Catholic, very devout, one who never missed church on Sundays. She encouraged me to believe in God but I just couldn't grasp it. "Jesus was a guy who got himself a good name for helping people," I thought. "But as for God himself, if He was there at all, which I doubted, He wasn't very good to me."

MARRIAGE

In November 1970 we were married. Norma's dad had promised us £500 as a wedding present and with half of that amount in our pockets we headed for London.

Sadly, marriage and its attendant responsibilities, didn't make me any wiser. After only a week in London I was again in trouble with the law, arrested for being in possession of an offensive weapon, an open razor.

For some reason I was released on bail of £25 and immediately went back to the same old wild ways. Norma went back up north to collect the rest of the money her dad had given us and, without her there to keep an eye on me, I played the fool. Every day, from morning to night, was one continuous binge of drink and drugs. Well, it was till the money was done.

DOUBLE CROSS

During that week I got into another big fight with men I was trying to buy drugs from. I thought they were trying to double-cross me so I threatened one of them with a knife. A brawl ensued with me, alone, against six of them. Standing at the corner of an entry I pelted them with empty milk bottles.

When the police arrived I didn't even try to escape. I stood there laughing and shouting obscenities at them. What did I care for them, or their rules and regulations? However, when they grabbed me, I struggled and fought against being hand-cuffed and bundled away.

At the court hearing the three magistrates were quite sympathetic to my case. I was charged with being in possession of an offensive weapon and of resisting arrest. My defence was that I had been attacked by a gang of youths and to protect myself till the police rescued me, I'd thrown the milk bottles at them. I was found not guilty on the charge of resisting arrest and given a conditional discharge for a year for carrying an offensive weapon.

At the end of the week Norma returned with the other £250 and I immediately went wild again. Within another week £200 had been blown on drink, drugs, clubs and wild living.

BREAK UP

Poor Norma didn't stand a chance with a character like me. After only eight days she gave up on me and went back home. Even as we said good-bye at Euston station she pleaded with me to go back with her. "We can still make it," she said, and begged me to change my mind. After promising to see her again in a few days, I hugged and kissed her farewell and watched the train depart.

In fact, I was never with her again. Our marriage had lasted eighteen days and through it all I had never shown her any consideration at all. Norma was completely without blame in the break up. It was all my fault. I suppose, in hindsight, we should never have married. It was a tragic mistake.

JUNKIE

After about six months I did return to Dumfries, but by this time I was a chronic alcoholic and a hopeless drug addict - a junkie. Any idea of settling down again with Norma was quickly abandoned.

Over the next two years I floated back and forth between Dumfries and London. I was always going to make it this time, I told myself. The sad truth is that in those two years I appeared in court on another five occasions. The charges were breach of the peace; possession of weapons; malicious damage; assault on the police and car theft. For these crimes I was handed further disqualifications from driving, fines, and two terms of imprisonment in Brixton prison.

Just before my twenty-third birthday I had another go at getting onto the straight and narrow. A catering agency got me a seasonal job in Guernsey, at a lovely hotel right on the sea front. Long golden sands stretched left and right almost as far as the eye could see. The weather, too, was marvellous.

My job as second chef didn't last long, however. When I discovered that drink on Guernsey wasn't taxed I couldn't believe my luck. Well, the temptation was too great to resist. I hit the bottle again - with a vengeance. The same old hatreds and vices reared themselves and within a few months I was behind bars again. This time it was as a guest of the Guernsey States prison, for fraud and theft.

HOME FROM HOME

What a great place that prison was. The food, prepared by the wives of the prison officers, was the nearest you could get to home cooking. The cells had under-floor heating and there was piped music too. It was like a holiday camp. I honestly didn't want to leave.

On release, I made immediately for Jersey, the largest of the Channel Isles. I got another job, this time in a small restaurant and again with living in accommodation. But the good times didn't last long there either. One evening, the restaurant owner came up to my room and informed me there were two detectives downstairs. They wanted to see me.

It turned out they had a warrant for my arrest on charges of theft. This was a job I thought I'd got away with. I'd taken a leather coat and £100 from a house in Streatham over a year ago. However, they'd caught up with me and they were taking me back.

Later that week, after a couple of overnights in the local Jersey prison, I was on the plane to London, accompanied by two C.I.D. men.

At the customs check in London the three of us walked straight through. I was hand-cuffed, of course, and one of the C.I.D. men held up his identity card. That meant no checks for us.

DUTY FREE!

An amusing incident occured when we arrived at the police station one of the officers opened my case and out popped cartons of cigarettes and bottles of whisky. Had the C.I.D. men had used my suit-case to smuggle through their undeclared goods? This incident further justified to my satisfaction, my intense dislike of the police.

After the brief court appearance, where I was released on bail of £25, I headed straight to Dumfries and home. After promising there would be no more trouble, my parents took me back in. Why they believed me I've no idea. Perhaps they didn't. Perhaps they were just proving the old adage that "blood is thicker than water."

Another fresh start was tried, this time at Butlin's Holiday Camp, near Ayr. In the mean time, I had been back to London to face the charges they had arrested me in Jersey for. I was given a £25 fine for one of them and got off on the other.

BUTLIN'S

At Butlin's the drink flowed freely every night and I usually ended up plastered. My job in the canteen required a five o'clock start every morning, but I wasn't getting to bed till about three. By seven o'clock every day I had to cook about 1000 eggs for the breakfasts. Beside the cooker there was a bin where we threw the egg shells. Many a morning I was sick into that bin half a dozen times. I wonder what the campers would have thought if they'd seen me?

As you've probably guessed, the Butlin's job lasted only a few weeks. I was fired for assaulting one of the chefs. This was to be the picture until the Lord finally took hold of me and changed my life. I drifted from town to town, all over England and Scotland, getting a good job in one catering establishment after another, only to loose it after a few weeks when the drink took control again.

This is the sad truth about drink or drug addiction; something that most doctors, psychiatrists and help agencies don't understand. No matter how much damage was being done to me by drink and no matter how much I wanted to give it up, and I did, I just couldn't. I was powerless in the grip of this evil master. It had full control.

Down, down I went in a never ending spiral of self destruction. However, it was just now that the first glimmerings of hope appeared on a distant horizon.

Believe on the Lord Jesus Christ and thou shalt be saved.

Acts 16:31

Chapter Thirteen

First Hope

The end of 1973 found me in jail again. This time it was the notorious Barlinnie prison in Glasgow. The atmosphere there was akin to the dark ages, I thought. The place was gloomy and cold, none of the clothes fitted, it was a recipe for misery and despair.

The cell itself was no parlour. Instead of a bed there was a piece of wood, about the size of a door, raised slightly from the floor. On top of it a mattress and a few blankets. In one corner there was a discoloured chamber pot, in the other, on a small table, stood a water jug and wash basin. Even the bar of soap was second hand.

Sunday morning came and there was a call along the corridor "Anyone for Bible Class?"

"Nothing else to do," I thought, and joined the line that paraded along to the prison chapel.

TESTIMONY

On the platform a group of young men and women sang songs about Jesus to the accompaniment of a couple of guitars. The main figure introduced himself as Willie Docherty, a travelling preacher. Willie gave · his testimony, telling us how Jesus had saved him from sin, changed his life and given him power to go and tell the good news of salvation to others. A few more songs from the young people and the meeting was over.

In my cell that night I lay and thought about what I had heard. Those young people seemed so happy, so assured, so confident. "How lucky they were," I thought. I wrestled with this for a long time, heard the words of Willie Docherty echoing through my mind again and again, and tried to make sense of them.

"You can be changed," he had told us. "You can be delivered from whatever powers grip you. You can be transformed. You can have a new life, and you can have peace. All this by getting to know this wonderful person Jesus, who died to save you."

But it was no use. Perhaps I didn't understand it properly. Perhaps I wasn't ready to let go and let God have his way. For what ever reason, I finally dismissed all I had heard as mere religious babble.

PEACE OF MIND?

Next day, in conversation with another prisoner, I explained that I'd been to the Bible Class and mentioned my troubled thoughts. He dismissed them and said that what they and every other religion claimed was a load of rubbish. "What we need is peace of mind," he said. It never struck me that that's exactly what I was looking for - and that's exactly what Willie Docherty and his young friends had promised.

A month after my Berlinnie stretch I was taken into the local psychiatric hospital to "dry out." My drinking habit was so bad now that I was buying cheap wine and mixing it with white spirit to give it more of a kick.

After three days I signed myself out. That was a daft thing to do because at least in the hospital there was a measure of warmth and shelter. But rational thought is far from the mind of someone so gripped by drink as I was.

BETHANY

On a Sunday evening in February 1974 I walked up Buccleugh Street, in Dumfries. It was raining, it was cold, and it was dark. The mood of the weather matched my spirits for I felt very ill and lonely.

Outside the Bethany Gospel Hall, I stopped for a moment and my eye caught the wording of the text displayed near the door. "By grace are ye saved!" it said.

A young woman appeared in the doorway at the top of the steps. "Would you like to come in?" she called.

"God wouldn't be looking for a character like me," I replied.

"God is looking for all kinds of people," she insisted, as she came down the steps towards me.

"My name's Fiona," she said. "What's yours?"

FIONA

I looked at her again in the half light of the street lamps. She was no film star, but there was a beauty, an inner attractiveness, a charm, and a sense of peace about her, such as I'd not seen in anyone for a long time. Her eyes portrayed a tenderness and love which told me that, even though she knew nothing about me, she cared.

I gave her my name and we stood chatting for a few minutes. Fiona spoke to me about the love of God, about the Saviour whom she knew personally and again invited me into the meeting. It seemed a better deal than walking the cold streets of Dumfries on a night like this, so I agreed.

Inside that little gospel hall the atmosphere was warm and cosy, the people friendly and happy, the singing bright and cheerful.

As the preacher stepped up to the lectern to deliver his sermon, I had it in my mind to prove him wrong. I wasn't going to take any of this "Jesus stuff," at face value. After all, what had Jesus done for me up till now?

CONVICTION

He was only about five minutes into his message when I began to see things more and more his way. I wondered if he knew something about me. Indeed, I wondered if he knew a lot about me.

For the first time ever, I saw how wicked my life had been. I began to feel remorse for the crimes I had committed. I saw how appalling my way of life had become. This man was getting through to me. It would be a while before I'd realise exactly what was happening - God was convicting me - but for the moment it shook me.

At the end of the meeting the preacher made an appeal to anyone who wanted spiritual help. I wanted to talk to this man. Maybe he could help me. He was very kind and sympathetic. He listened to my tale of woe and assured me that Jesus could change my life.

"You need to be saved," he told me.

"How does that happen?" I asked.

"By receiving Jesus Christ as your personal saviour," he replied.

"Let's do it," I said.

"Do you mean it?" he asked.

"Yes I do," I affirmed - and I meant it.

ON MY KNEES

Along with two other men from the church we went into another, more private room. After a lot of questions to make sure I understood what I was doing we all knelt down together. Following the preacher as he led in prayer I confessed my sins to Jesus and asked him to come into my heart and life.

The prayer was over in just a few moments and I rose from my knees with a new sense of happiness. We sat talking for a while as they gave me some help with living the Christian life. Then they bade me God speed and wished me well for the future. Of course, they did ask me to come and see them again.

A HOLY JOE?

Alas, after only two days I met a drinking pal of mine and with the minimum of encouragement went back into the pub with him. Over a pint we talked about what had happened at the Gospel Hall. "Don't worry yourself about that," he said. "As long as you believe you'll go to heaven you'll be all right. You don't have to become a Holy Joe or a Bible basher when you're a Christian. A lot of these people who go to meetings all the time are religious fanatics."

I have to admit that the more drink we consumed the more his ides appealed to me. Perhaps these folk were a bit too religious for me.

"Surely, as long as I believe I can do more or less what I want," I reasoned. The next five years were to prove just what a foolish philosophy that was.

IN TROUBLE AGAIN.

One week after the Gospel Hall experience I stood in the dock at the local Sheriff's Court charged with "breach of the peace." Another two months in Barlinnie was the outcome. The first night there I lay in the cell and rolled a cigarette. Only a few weeks earlier I'd lain in an adjacent cell and vowed I'd never be back again. But here I was.

On release I went to my dad's shop where he kitted me out in a new suit and a fine pair of dress boots. "How about a drink?" he enquired. That sounded good to me so off we sauntered to the pub, me feeling quite a dandy in my new gear.

Without going into detail, it's sufficient to say that, after a few drinks, a brawl developed in the pub. I thought a man was coming at me with a glass, to injure me, so I turned on him and shoved a glass into his face. The upshot was that he ended up on the floor needing an ambulance. I was hand-cuffed and carted off to a police cell yet again.

THE BIG ONE

When the desk sergeant brought my breakfast next morning he said "Well John, this is the big one. You're for a long stretch this time lad. At least ten years."

The threat of "ten years," was, in a way, good news. I knew at least that Rab, the guy I had clobbered, wasn't dead. If he'd been dead the sergeant would have threatening me with "life."

He told me I was being charged with attempted murder and then he added. "Pity you hadn't killed him. Then we would have been rid of two pieces of scum at the same time."

As he walked away laughing I hurled curses and abuse at him.

My case was heard in private and lasted all of two minutes. I would spend another four months in the dreaded Barlinnie jail. Another four months to consider my pitiful existence - to repent, if I could, of the life I was leading.

ALL A DREAM?

In my cell that first night in Barlinnie the consideration began. My thought went back again to that night in the Gospel Hall. Was it all a dream? Did I really ask Jesus into my heart that night - and was I sincere?

"If you are there, Lord Jesus, please help me," was my short muttered prayer.

Next day I was told that the charge of attempted murder had been reduced to "assault to cause severe injury." Two days later it was further reduced to "assault." The day after it was reduced again, this time to "breach of the peace." Rab was also charged.

I was immediately released on £25 bail put up by my dad and left Barlinnie surprised and amazed.

SHOW TIME!

It was Rab who gave me the full story behind these alterations in the charges. He'd had a row with my dad over a record player. My dad had threatened to have him "sorted out," by me. So when Rab saw me in the pub he thought this was "show time." That's why he went for me.

Rab wouldn't charge me, so the police had no case. When it eventually came to court the trial was abandoned and we both went free.

In the next three years I served three more terms in Barlinnie. Each would be my last, I vowed.

However, each time I was "put away," my thoughts returned to this person Jesus Christ. There seemed to be a battle raging within me ever since the Gospel Hall encounter. One part of me desperately wanted to be for Jesus. The other part of me wanted to lap up the pleasures of sin.

TWO DOGS

I was like the simple old preacher who gave the illustration of his own earlier life as a young believer. He said that it was as if there were two dogs inside him. One wanted to be good, docile, friendly and faithful to his master. The other wanted to bite the postman, worry sheep and make a nuisance of himself. "Which one wins?" someone asked him.

"The one I feed the most," he admitted. It was clear to me that I was feeding the wrong dog.

For me, it was like living with God and the Devil at the same time. Time after time I told God that I didn't want his son in my life. Thankfully, He didn't listen to my foolish requests. Thankfully, He is a God of mercy, of compassion and of grace.

The inner battle reached such a climax at times that I felt I could kill someone in an effort to get peace of mind. The notion was foolish, of course, but that's the way my tortured mind worked. Night after night I lay in my little cell trying to work out the answers to the questions that perplexed me.

THE CROSS

One day I took a piece of chalk from the prison laundry where I worked. That evening, after the "pass man," had been round with the pail of tea and there was little chance of me being disturbed, I drew a large cross on one wall of my cell. Kneeling down before it I asked God to forgive all my sins and to grant me peace of mind.

I stayed on my knees till ten o'clock, when the guard came and turned of the lights. Later, in bed, I promised God that when I was released I would serve Him. Unfortunately, the path of destiny would put that promise on hold for a while yet.

Chapter Fourteen

TO LONDON AGAIN

The beginning of 1975 saw me off to London again - for yet another fresh start. My eldest brother had a house in Shepherd's Bush and he invited me to stay with him. This had a kind of stabilising effect - at least for a while.

I got a job in a restaurant near the Cafe Royal, in Picadilly. It paid well so I was comfortable - honestly comfortable - at last.

My experiences in the restaurant gave me a wonderful insight into another world - the world of stardom and the movies. Leicester Square was just across from the restaurant and its cinemas were often the venues for big film premiers.

Afterwards a lot of the celebrities would pile into our restaurant - specially booked - for a bit of a celebration. Michael Caine, Diana Dors, Rupert Davis were just some of the big stars that I, as a humble waiter, met at these parties.

STARS

I call them parties. They were more like pantomimes, all sham and humbug, all hypocrisy and falseness. The conduct and language of many of these "celebrities," was shocking in the extreme and dramatically altered my opinion of them. One thing became very clear to me. There is no real difference between a rich alcoholic and a poor one. They are both headed for a drunkard's grave.

But, while I was making these observations on the lives of others - and secretly denouncing their lurid conduct - there was no change in my own life. In fact, the downgrade continued.

A fair bit of cash had been saved up and I was preparing myself for another drinking binge. However, even in the midst of these preparations my thoughts continually harked back to spiritual matters. There was a conscious feeling of guilt within me, a guilt which couldn't be dismissed, not even diminished, by anything I did. I was still determined to believe in God, but it was going to be on my terms, my way, or so I fancied.

To rid myself of these troubled thoughts I embarked on a wild spree of the pubs, clubs and discos of London. Anywhere that pleasure could be found, I'd be there searching for it. I was spending a fortune, it seemed to me, on drink, massage parlours, women and drugs. When money ran low I stole and resold to top up the diminished coffers.

Bad company came my way on these flings. People of ill repute weren't hard to find, but I seemed so particularly adept at finding them. Once, on the green opposite the BBC's Shepherd's Bush studios, I spent three whole days in a drunken stupor. Every time I tried to leave the green someone handed me a bottle of cheap wine, meths, white spirit, or even hair lacquer to swig from. This kept me in a paralytic state. I was only rescued when the police came and picked me up on yet another theft charge.

PENTONVILLE

This time it was Pentonville prison, a place which has saved the lives of countless numbers of men. Many hopeless cases would be dead today were it not for the fact that they were put away behind the walls of Pentonville for a while. Sadly, like every prison, it's a breeding ground for crime too.

A man in Pentonville gave me an address and asked me to deliver a message when I got out to the person who lived there. This guy became a great friend of mine and we embarked on a handy little scam together.

At lunch times we visited building sites and, when the men were in their portakabins having a bite to eat and enjoying a few hands of cards we'd help ourselves to anything we saw.

Hand tools, buzz saws, items of portable equipment, all were easily disposed of and the money helped to feed our drink and drugs habits.

After one particularly good week at this racket I ended up in a pub in Streatham, in South West London. There was a bulge of notes in my hip pocket and I was eager to spend it.   Very soon I was drinking black rum, like a pirate. It didn't take long for the lethal liquor to induce pirate behaviour.

At the table beside, me three young skin-heads sat drinking. We got into conversation. I took exception to the Swastikas tattooed on their foreheads. Very soon a row developed and the open razors flashed again, cutting into them. The police were called and that's when the fun really started.

ANOTHER BRAWL

Kicking and screaming I was dragged from the bar towards the Black Maria. Try as they might they couldn't get me into the van. I was batoned, kicked and punched to the ground time and time again. Each time I got up again as fierce as before. A crowd gathered to witness the spectacle and the rougher the fighting the more they cheered. Eventually the police gave up and half dragged, half shoved me the short distance to the station. Despite being handcuffed, I kicked and struggled all the way.

Once inside, they made the foolish mistake of removing the cuffs. Immediately I lashed out again attacking a young policeman and starting a whole new battle. With someone calling over the din "Take it easy, you'll kill him!" they set to with batons, fists and feet again. Unconsciousness saved me from further beating.

I woke up in the cell completely naked and hand-cuffed again. A policeman sat on the edge of the bed and when he saw me stir he called out "Hey Sarge, he's coming round!"

The cell door swung wide and the sergeant enquired "How is he, the mad b———. Is he sober enough to be finger printed? We must find out who he is.

Someone brought an old police shirt and a pair of ill fitting trousers. "Put these on." I was told. "We're taking you upstairs for finger prints. If you behave yourself we'll give you a cup of tea and let you have a smoke. But mind you, no nonsense!"

WORLD WAR II

The whole scene was redolent of a World War 2 movie. During it all I had remained completely silent, refusing even to recognise my captors. I was seething within but I wasn't going to let them know it.

They walked me along a corridor with glass doors on each side. All was going quietly, with the police lulled into a false sense of security. Suddenly I broke free and jumped straight through one of the doors, sending splinters of glass flying in all directions.

A young policeman sat at a desk, typing. When the glass crashed around him and I appeared he stood up, horror stricken. Picking myself up from the floor I butted him full in the face and, as he hit the floor, picked up the typewriter intending to hurl it through the window. I never did because there was a dull thud on the back of my head, the familiar pattern of stars, and blackout.

When I woke up this time I was lying on a soft floor with my hands firmly fixed to my chest. As full consciousness returned it became clear that I was in a padded cell and in a straight-jacket. "They don't still have these things?" I thought. But no, I wasn't dreaming. I was trussed like a turkey and all alone in this strange little room.

GOD AGAIN

My thoughts drifted back to Dumfries and that lovely Christian girl I had met at the Bethany Gospel Hall. "God looks for all kinds of men," she had told me. "Was He still looking for me?" I wondered. And then I cried "Please God, help me."

One wall of the room swung inwards. It was, in fact, the door opening. Two figures in white coats stood there, one of them holding a tray of food.

"Well then my friend, what's it all about?" enquired one of them. He approached and began to untie the straight jacket. "Let's have something to eat, shall we?" His tone was patronising. The second man came nearer with the tray of food and when he got within range I lunged out with one foot and kicked the tray high into the air, scattering its contents to the four padded walls.

"I'm not a child!" I screamed, and added "Get out of here and leave me alone."

THE NEEDLE

At this point a large black man appeared. He was also garbed in white and, more importantly, was armed with a menacing looking hypodermic needle. The first two men held me down, the black man came forward, there was a sharp prick in my buttock - and darkness!

I've no idea how much time passed before I regained consciousness, but when I did I just lay there staring at those pale padded walls. Eventually, a doctor appeared, along with the two nurses I'd abused. The doctor spoke. What he had to say was terse and had a finality about it.

"You must be sick of that straight jacket. But all this violence won't help you get out of here. Do you realise why you're here? You're on a 72 hour test. If we find you insane, you stay. If we decide that your sane, you go. But it's all up to you, young man!"

This stunned me. Prison was one thing, the somersault factory, as we called it, was another. "This was the big one," I thought. The police hand you over to the mental hospital because they're pretty sure you won't make it through the 72 hour sanity test. If they're right they have no more bother with you.

Prison and the mental hospital differed dramatically. In prison you spent your time in the company of people of your own type and social class. In the asylum there were all sorts. Drug addicts, who had taken a trip too far. Refugees from the flower power age of the sixties. Poor souls who had stuffed their arms so full of heroin they lost their veins - and their brains. Then there were the schizophrenics, the psychopaths and those who were paranoid. I couldn't imagine spending my time with a bunch of "nutcases," so I set myself to some serious thinking.

TRICK CYCLISTS

I had three days to convince these "trick-cyclists," the psychiatrists, that I hadn't gone over the horizon. Could I do it?

At the first session with the doctors I had to be careful to repeat the lies I had already told them. I had given my name as John Scott and, to my surprise they believed me. That name was even written on my bed chart.

The two hour session seemed like two weeks, with a never ending stream of questions. How well did I get on with my parents? When I was a boy did I play marbles? Did I have any sexual fetishes? "What would they ask me next?"

Back in the doctor's office he asked me if I'd ever been in trouble with the police before. "Never!" I lied. To my surprise I was set free on the condition that I attended the hospital three times a week for counselling. That was the last they saw of me. I never returned.

WRESTLING

About a year had passed since my Bethany Hall experience. I remember my 24th birthday particularly. The thoughts about God were constantly with me. Inside, the struggle continued - me wrestling with God and, I suppose - God wrestling with me. I wanted to be a better man but I always seemed to end up doing the exact opposite to what I wanted. I was, in the words of the apostle Paul "a servant of sin." That sums it up.

In May 1975 Scotland's Tartan Army invaded Wembley Soccer Stadium for an England Scotland football match. Since the car crash years earlier, when my feet were broken, I had hated the game - and still did. However, this would be an excuse for a good booze up, so I joined a crowd of my mates in front of a TV set to watch the big match. It resulted in Scotland being trounced five goals to one. That, in turn, led to a night on the town drowning our sorrows.

We finished up in a club in Notting Hill Gate with a disc jockey in one corner pumping out loud dance music and an atmosphere thick with cigarette smoke. As usual, a brawl ensued. And, as usual, I was in the thick of it. However, without having to call the police, the club bouncers managed to quell the disturbance.

At about three o'clock in the morning I was making my way out of the club down a flight of stairs. My two mates had gone to collect our coats and to buy some cigarettes, so as I staggered down the steps with half a bottle of rum under one arm, I was alone.

"JUST HANG ON!"

Suddenly a sharp, searing pain gripped my chest. The bottle of rum smashed to the pavement and both my hands clutched by breast. The warm flow of my own blood seeping through my fingers confirmed that I'd been stabbed. I had neither heard nor seen my attackers.

Now they were face to face with me and moving in for what seemed like the kill. They danced before me like two mystical, dark figures from a ghost story. Again and again they stabbed at me, knifing me first in the shoulder, then three times in the back, and finally, in the side. Then, as quickly as they had appeared, they were gone into the darkness.

Falling to my knees I gasped what I believed were my last breaths on earth and sunk into unconsciousness. The next thing I was aware of was the faint, distant sound of sirens. The sirens became louder. Blurred vision gave way to clearer sight and the presence of my two friends and a stranger leaning over me. "You're going to be all right John. Just hang on!" they pleaded.

THE GRIM REAPER!

As the ambulance bumped and swayed its way to hospital their words were of little comfort. My mind was on something far more important; far more serious and immediate. I was staring into the jaws of death and the sight terrified me. All my worldly possessions, few as they were; all my mates and girlfriends; all the fun I'd had; all my hopes, fears, dreams and religious knowledge vanished in the face of the picture that confronted me.

The Bethany Hall experience, the girl at the top of the steps, the meeting inside, the preaching of the gospel, asking Christ into my heart afterwards - "was it real," I wondered. "Will I go to Heaven or Hell?" This was the question that was uppermost in my mind now. And I wasn't sure of the answer. Inwardly I prayed "Please God, take me into your care. Don't let me go to Hell." Then darkness again.

Chapter Fifteen

GOD SEEKS ME AGAIN

The door of the pure white hospital ward opened and the biggest black lady I've ever seen waddled towards me. "How're you feelin' Mr. Wilson?" she called out cheerily. "Seems you got yourself stabbed a few times, but your goin' to be all right."

It turned out I was in the intensive care unit of the local hospital. There were tubes down each nostril, tubes in my arms, and tubes in places I'd rather not mention. I was plumbed like a washing machine and there were bottles and drips hanging everywhere. But the main thing, the great thing was - I was alive!

The door opened again and a doctor came in. After asking how I felt, he proceeded to give me a complete assessment of my condition. I'd been stabbed six times. The knife had penetrated my left kidney, very slightly, and just missed my heart. Surgery may be needed for both these wounds and the kidney may have to be removed. But there was no need for worry. The chest wound was a simple operation and, if the kidney had to be sacrificed, I could live quite well with just one.

NO DANGER

"But don't worry Mr. Wilson. You're off the danger list and you'll soon be moved through to the main ward." With that, he left as quickly as he had entered. "What did I tell you, Mr. Wilson. You're goin' to be fine," cooed the big, black nurse, who was still hovering nearby - and she smiled a long row of pearly white teeth at me.

During the next week those troubling thoughts about God came to haunt me again and again. On a few occasions I prayed. It was the old story again - when everything was going fine, God was forgotten, but when the chips were down I turned to search for Him again.

ANOTHER FIONA

One day, after about a week in the hospital, a young nurse came to see me. Her badge told me her name was Fiona. "Hello Mr. Wilson," she said, "we're going to wheel you through to the main ward."

She was very attractive and something about her seemed familiar. While we waited for a porter to come and help her, we chatted together. The hospital was St. Mary's on the Harrow Road and she'd been there for about a year. Her surname was McIntosh, she said, and she was from Scotland. Quite politely and sincerely, she told me how she's come to know the Lord seven years before. She seemed radiant with the joy of God's salvation and, in a way, I envied her.

My Bethany Hall encounter came to mind and I told her about my making a profession of faith in Jesus. "Did you mean it," she asked. "Of course I meant it," I replied. "It's coming to terms with it that's causing me trouble. I can't seem to break away from my way of living. With all my heart I want to serve God, but time after time I go back to drink, drugs and all the other wickedness associated with them. It would take me all day to tell you about the wicked things I've done," I confessed.

"Listen," Fiona interjected, "my friend who is also a nurse here is a Christian too. Would you like us to visit you from time to time? We could come both on and off duty."

"That would be great," I said, and I really meant it.

SET BACK

A few days later I suffered a set back and had to undergo surgery for the problem with the damaged kidney. Waking up after the operation was a lovely experience, though. As my eyes dreamily became accustomed to the surroundings of the ward, who was there bending over me and whispering assurance but the lovely Fiona?

"It's all right John. The Lord has brought you through. Our small fellowship has prayed all night for your safety and the Lord has heard our prayers.

I was touched by Fiona's kindness and amazed that a group of people who didn't know me would stay up all night to pray for a wretch like me. In later years,I came to realise this as practical Christianity in action.

Fiona continued, "You won't be needing any more surgery John. The wound in your chest is healing up fine and we're well pleased with your progress."

"I wish," I replied, "that God was well pleased with my progress."

A few days later Fiona and her friend came to see me in their off duty clothes. "You're the second Fiona to come in to my life," I said. "And the other one was a Christian too. I told her again about the Bethany Hall experience."

"We're going to Rome, on holiday, next week," Fiona informed me. "We'll send you a card. Maybe that'll cheer you up a bit." And true to her word, she did.

Her kindness, her thoughtfulness made me even more determined to be a Christian. I was to learn, however, that it took something far removed from determination to make a person a follower of Christ.

A GLIMPSE OF THE GRIM REAPER

Just before I was discharged from St. Mary's, something happened which brought home to me with greater effect than anything I'd ever witnessed, the necessity of being a true believer in the Lord Jesus.

The man in the bed opposite to mine suddenly began wheezing and gasping for breath. Very quickly, the nurses wheeled in the oxygen trolley, held the mask to his face and opened the valve to allow the precious gas to flow. Through a chink in the curtains I could see all that was happening. The man's breathing improved almost immediately, so much so, that the nurses decided to leave him. They put his hand to the mask, spoke a few words of reassurance and slipped away.

I watched him lying there, holding the mask to his mouth and breathing softly and slowly. I had come to know him quite well. I met his wife and daughter too. The daughter often brought me magazines and fruit, and sat and chatted with me while the old man and her mother talked alone.

As I peered at him through the gap in the curtains his breathing stopped. The mask fell from his grip, rolling silently on to his chest. His eyes stared coldly ahead. His body was motionless. The old man was dead.

In less than five minutes, he had been lifted on to a metal trolley and wheeled away to the morgue. The bed linen was changed, the locker emptied, a burst of air freshener sprayed around and the curtains drawn back. Before another five minutes had passed, another patient was in the bed.

"Is this all the value they place on life?" I thought. "Is this how cheap it is - and how short?

Chapter Sixteen

EVER DOWNWARD

The last person I spoke to, before being discharged from hospital the following morning was the lovely Fiona. As she wished me well, I promised her faithfully that I'd see her in the gospel meeting the next Sunday.

Five minutes later, I was in a pub less than a hundred yards from the hospital. In less than two hours, I was roaring drunk. So drunk, in fact, that the police were called for and I was carted off again, under arrest.

Next morning, on the way to court, I had to ask what the charge was this time. I'd been so drunk I didn't know what I was doing, or what I had done. When they told me it was theft I breathed a great sigh of relief. Considering the state I was in, it could have been murder.

My excuse was that I was just out of hospital and had been stupid enough to take drink on top of medication. It was a clever try, but it didn't keep me out of Pentonville.

BANK ROBBERS

Back out again, I teamed up with a Londoner by the name of Pete. We met in a bar in Paddington and the more I got to know him the more I realised what a bad guy he was.

Anyway, after a few arguments and fights we eventually had each other sized up and became quite good friends. Such good friends, in fact, that we decided to go into business together - as bank robbers!

Success at bank robbery requires one essential piece of equipment - a gun. We didn't have one. However, on a building site where we'd taken work for a while, there were a couple of men who said they'd find us the right weapon.

Next day they handed us an oily rag with something heavy wrapped in it. It was a .38 calibre Smith & Wesson revolver. It came with a box of shells too.

That night, at the back of Pete's house, we had our first target practice. The noise of the revolver firing could be heard all along the street. Everybody knew what was going on, but nobody bothered us, and nobody called the police.

While waiting for the chance to do our first bank robbery I heard some rather interesting news. One of the guys who had stabbed me, coming out the pub in the darkness, was out on bail pending trial at the Old Bailey for attempted murder.

REVENGE!

Now that I had access to a gun it seemed to me that I could get revenge, in a very dramatic way. A few nights later, when I was well tanked up, it seemed that the opportune moment had come.

At Pete's house I got hold of the gun, loaded it with bullets, and announced that I was going to find that b_____ who had cut me up, and blow him away. Pete and a girlfriend of mine remonstrated with me, pointing out that it wasn't worth it. I'd be caught in the end and put away for years.

Heedless of their warnings, I stormed out and headed for the pub, for one more glass of Dutch courage. Tonight I'd show them what kind of man I really was.

With the gun tucked securely in my waist-band I felt all powerful. The truth is, I was probably close to insanity.

DUTCH COURAGE

At the pub, more than a few glasses of Dutch courage were consumed. As the drink took effect, I became more and more intent on using the gun. I wanted to shoot someone. I wanted to shoot anyone!

Forgetting, for the moment, the murder plans, I hopped on a tube for Acton. I had two old pals there and I thought I'd pay them a surprise visit.

Sitting in the tube station at Shepherd's Bush, waiting for the train, I was overcome with thoughts of violence. "I must use this gun," I thought. "I know. I'll shoot the first person who steps off the next train that pulls into the station."

Moments later, the distant rumble of an approaching train was followed by the squeak of metal wheel on metal rail, and then the whoosh of wind as the train thundered out of the tunnel towards the platform.

My hand closed firmly around the gun. As I drew it slowly from my waistband, I pulled back the hammer with my thumb.

The train stopped and the hiss of air brakes was followed by the rattle of a dozen sliding doors opening simultaneously.

I raised the gun to take aim, taking up the pressure on the trigger.

"I'll shoot the first person who steps off the train." The words echoed through my head.

A CLOSE CALL

The first person to step off the train was a Jamaican gentleman. Pointing the gun at him I followed him with my aim and tightened the pressure on the trigger. Keeping him in the sights I squeezed the trigger harder and harder. My hands trembled with a mixture of fear and excitement. I half closed my eyes in expectation of the flash which would follow the explosion. I wanted to cover my ears because I knew a gunshot would be deafening in this enclosed space. But nothing happened. I just couldn't go through with it. The Jamaican gentleman walked off the platform, through one of the archways, and out of my life, ignorant of all that had taken place between him and me. I wasn't such a hard man after all. I'll be eternally grateful that the gun was never fired. I shudder to think of the consequences. But it was a close call.

After visiting my friends in Acton I hailed a cab to take me back to Pete's house. About two hundred yards from the house I asked the taxi driver to let me off. "That'll be £2," he said. Jumping out quickly, I went round to his door, as if to pay him. Instead, I stuck the gun in through his open window and pointed it at his face.

"Give me your money or I'll blow your head off your shoulders," I threatened. He fumbled in his pockets for a moment and thrust a handful of notes into my hand. Grabbing it, I stumbled off down back streets and entries, heading for Pete's.

Very quickly the alarm was raised, the sound of police sirens adding speed to my run for Pete's.

I got there just before the peelers and, with a bit of help from Pete and a few other friends, managed to escape their clutches. However, since the heat was on, I thought it best to get out of London.

HOME AGAIN

The journey from Euston station to Dumfries took five hours. As the train pulled into the station of my home town, my spirits were at a low ebb. Dumfries was home. I liked the place. But my record of crime was so bad there was hardly anywhere I could go, and nowhere to hide.

I was only home three weeks when, walking down the street one day with my girlfriend, the police caught up with me.

"Right John. Up against the wall son." The young, eager detective had jumped from the police car which had just screeched to a halt beside me. He was accompanied by an equally eager and tough sergeant, and a young constable.

After the spread-eagled search they bundled me into the back of the car and sped off to the local police station. My girlfriend stood on the pavement, eyes agog.

"What's this about a robbery in London then, John?" The question came from a plain clothes detective. He was accompanied by a uniformed constable and the inspector.

"Don't know what you're talking about," I retorted.

"Oh come on John," he snapped. "We have two witnesses who tell us they heard you talk about this in the Whitesands Inn."

Using the choicest of language, I told him what I thought of his witnesses - and what he could do with them.

The detective made a move for me. I assumed he was intent on jogging my memory with a few wallops about the head. But the inspector stopped him.

"Look John," he intoned. "Come clean. We know all about the gun, and the taxi being robbed. We know where it happened, near Paddington. The police in London have been in touch with us and we have a warrant for your arrest."

A long argument ensued. The police threatened me with everything in the book. I told them to get lost, although not quite so politely as that.

BACK TO LONDON

The upshot was that I was taken back to London, by plane, between two officers. There I faced very serious charges in connection with possession of the gun.

The police were very anxious to get the names of the men who had sold us the gun. Apparently, (and I didn't know this at the time), we did the deal with two Irishmen whom the police thought had some connection with the I.R.A. There were bombings in London at the time and a lot of guns were in circulation, so I suppose it's no surprise there were I.R.A. connections somewhere along the line.

In Brixton prison I was on an identity parade and picked out by the taxi driver. Also while there, I was visited by police who had been looking for me in connection with the stabbing incident, outside the pub. They were going to call me as a witness against the two men they had picked up for that attempt on my life.

Entering the witness box at the Old Bailey, it was clear that the two men in the dock were the guys who had attacked me. I was asked to identify them, but refused. That is, I pretended that it was so dark on that night in Notting Hill, and I was so intent on defending myself, that I didn't get a good look at them.

HONOUR AMONG THIEVES

I don't think the court believed me, but without my testimony against the men, there was nothing they could do. The prosecution council was visibly shaken, and inwardly seething, I should think. He had been expecting a conviction on the strength of my evidence.

After the court hearing we were cuffed together in pairs. To my surprise I was cuffed to one of the men whom I'd been asked to testify against, one of the men who had stabbed me. I say I was surprised. He was shocked!

He began to babble apologies, fearing, I think, that I'd be out for my usual revenge. I reminded him that all the apologies in the world wouldn't bring back the kidney I had lost, and told him to shut up and to forget it. For once, I really meant it.

Chapter Seventeen

THE SAME OLD STORY

The next few years followed the pattern of the ones before. I was into drink, drugs, burglary, petty (and sometimes not so petty) theft, and anything else that would support the life style I had become accustomed to. In tandem with that, there were the frequent spells in prison.

Wandsworth was where they put me after the Old Bailey experience. Amongst criminals, it has the worst reputation of all London prisons. The discipline is rigid and regimental. Everything happens strictly according to the rules - and the rules are harsh. The screws (prison officers) act like sergeant majors, suffering no attempts at bending the rules. One false move and the prisoner is on report.

THE SALVATION ARMY

On admission to Wandsworth I'd been asked, as usual, what religion I was. Just to be smart, I said "Salvationist." The joke backfired on me- for a few days later, the cell door swung open and in walked a Salvation Army Captain.

He greeted me with a cheery "Praise the Lord, brother." To my own surprise I replied with "Hallelujah!"

He marched over to me and said "You know, the Lord loves you brother. Will you come to our Christmas service on Sunday?"

He was the only person who had spoken to me in a friendly manner for weeks, so what could I do but agree.

When he left, after half an hour, he gave me copies of "The War Cry," and "Young Soldier." Normally I'd have chucked them away, but this time I read them both from cover to cover.

STILL SEARCHING

The weeks in Wandsworth passed quickly. This was because I spent most of my time reading. I was still searching. What I was searching for I wasn't sure, but I was searching. I read books on Zen Buddhism, Catholicism, Mormonism; books on the Jehovah's Witnesses, the Gurus, the Dervishes and the Eastern Cults; and books on Jewish Law, philosophy, science, evolution and transcendental meditation.

All these volumes claimed to have the answers to the problems of mankind, but none of them provided the answers to mine. After reading them, I was still searching.

At the end of each week I liked nothing better than to make my way to the room at the top of the spiral staircase. This was where the Salvation Army held their Sunday meetings. About a half a dozen old men, and myself were all that attended, but despite this there was always a feel good factor about those times. Apart from the genuine kindness of the Captain who led the meetings, I remember that the singing always made a very strong impression on me. It made me feel warm inside.

The Captain and myself had some long and beneficial conversations. He was a very patient and gracious man, and always had time to answer all the questions I put to him. Looking back, I'm sure he was one of the vital links in my eventual finding of the true path to life and salvation.

However, at the time, despite all his patience, and the clarity of his instruction, I just couldn't grasp the basic realities of salvation. There were far too many questions - and far too many answers. It was all beyond my comprehension.

CANNABIS

Just before I left Wandsworth another inmate managed to smuggle some cannabis resin to me. I was in a single cell. That made detection much more difficult. For one thing, when you do things by yourself, and keep them to yourself, there's nobody to "grass" on you.

So each night, after the 7.30pm cup of tea, I "skinned-up" as we say and smoked a "spliff." Cannabis is amazing stuff, with amazing effects on the human mind.

I sat in my cell for hours at a time, inhaling the aroma of this powerful drug, and fully contemplating all the things I had read. I don't know that I ever came to any earth shattering conclusions, but if I'm honest I'll have to say I enjoyed the experience - at the time.

To be honest again, the cannabis experiences weren't always as good as I've described them. I was leaving Wandsworth in a couple of days, so, as a kind of a celebration I had rolled and tucked away a couple of joints of a specially powerful cannabis - "Afghanistan Black."

When the last check up for the night had been made, I lit up. After a few draws my thoughts began to turn to God. I began talking to Him, and praying. "Please God, if you're really there, let me be aware of you." The more I smoked, the more enlightened I felt. "This is a wonderful experience," I thought. "I hope it lasts forever."

DEMONS

It continued like this until the night guard put out the light. Suddenly, I began to hallucinate in the most weird and frightening fashion. Black demons, ghouls and devils invaded my thoughts. It seemed my cell was full of them. A great fear took hold of me and I began praying again in desperation. "Please God, don't let them get hold of me. Protect me!"

This was one of the most terrifying experiences of my life. Dope smoking was a great escape from reality, but when it went wrong, it nearly drove me mad. There were other side effects too. It made me irritable, self-conscious, very nervous and paranoid.

All that night I lay awake, longing, praying, waiting for the dawn to come, with its welcome light. Next Sunday morning I was back in that upper room with the Salvation Army, singing the praises of God.

ON THE ISLE OF WIGHT

From Wandsworth I was moved to Parkhurst, on the Isle of Wight. There were some really hardened cases in that place; child molesters, murderers and one or two who had shot policemen. Most of these men were in for life. "What a waste," I thought.

Late in 1976, I was released from Parkhurst, and given a one-way ticket to Dumfries.

Leaving the island on the ferry, my thoughts raced back over the past nineteen months. What had prison done for me in that time? Well, I'd read a lot of books, and so increased my knowledge. I'd learned to control my temper - that had to be good. I'd learned to relate better to people, especially from different cultural and ethnic backgrounds, like the black men I'd been imprisoned with.

But, as I watched the seagulls wheeling and diving around the ship on that crisp November morning, all these "accomplishments" seemed decidedly irrelevant now. I pushed the memories far from my mind and went back to watching the seagulls.

That didn't last long as thoughts of the past overcame me again. It was almost three years since my Bethany Hall profession. It still nagged at my innermost being. The "Why," questions re-surfaced. There were so many whys. Why did I drink so much? Why couldn't I be a better man? Why was the world such an unfair place? Why were there wars? Why was it so hard to believe in Jesus? And - why didn't God help me?

Portsmouth - and the ferry drew alongside the dock. I hung back to allow the other passengers to disembark. I would savour this coming ashore - like some home-coming hero. Who was I fooling?

I strolled down the gang-plank, and ashore, taking all the time in the world. Then, without having to slink from hiding to hiding, and without having to look over my shoulder in case a policeman might be following, I made my way to catch the train to Waterloo.

"THE ONLY WAY TO BE SAVED!"

Just as I was about to step on to the train something lying on the platform caught my eye. I bent down and picked it up. It was a gospel tract. For the first ten minutes of that journey to Waterloo "The Only Way to be Saved," kept me occupied. It explained how man was lost through sin and out of touch with God. And it told of how Jesus came from Heaven, to die on the cross and to be the Saviour to mankind. All I had to do was believe and receive Him by faith. It all seemed so simple, and it all seemed so clear.

After a few cans of beer in the buffet-car, however, I soon forgot the message of the tract and turned my thoughts to more mundane matters.

TRAIN ROBBER

The face of the flower seller at Waterloo station was instantly recognisable.

"Hello Buster. How're you doin'?" I called out. "Well Jock, me old mate, how's it goin' for you son?" he replied cheerily.

"Just out this mornin' Buster. That's another one finished."

"Take my advice, make it your last, Jock. You can't beat the system." There was a sombre note in his voice as he passed on his advice.

If any man should know that you can't beat the system, it was Buster. He had been involved in the now famous, great train robbery. He had been one of the "clean up" men, and now, after ten and a half years behind bars, here he was standing at Waterloo Station selling flowers. Perhaps surprisingly, the thought that struck me was that Buster was much better off selling flowers than taking foolish chances in the hope of greater riches.

Chapter Eighteen

DESTINY?

In a few hours the train would pull into Dumfries, my home town. "What had destiny in store for me this time?" I wondered. In the past ten years I'd left home on more than a dozen occasions with the sincere hope that, from here on, things would be different; better. Each time, it had turned out to be a forlorn hope. Each time I'd crawled back home to Dumfries a failure.

Here I was at the age of twenty-six and what a sorry mess I was in. Crippled, minus a kidney, addicted to drink and drugs, divorced, a list of convictions as long as your arm, and a string of prison sentences to my shame. And that's only part of the picture.

Like a quick change artist on a stage, I could discard one mask and don another, in moments. Now, all the control and calmness I'd demonstrated over the past months melted away. A great bitterness gripped me as I considered my situation. The violent nature and the aggressive attitude were just under the surface, waiting to be unleashed at the slightest provocation.

It didn't take long, and it didn't take much for the excuse of provocation to be used. I was only in Dumfries a couple of days when I got into a bar-room brawl, just because I thought another guy was looking at me too much. He wasn't, but that didn't stop me having a go at him.

My life of crime continued, especially, when I was put in a position of trust.

SELF CATERING

An ex-prison mate of mine got me a job in a hotel in Dumfries. The manager knew nothing of my past and gave me the key of the wine cellar. Naturally, I began helping my self to the stock. I stole food too, chickens, packets of scampi and steaks. What I didn't use myself, I sold. With the wine, the food and the money I made from selling the residue, my girlfriend, Julie, and myself lived in fine style for months. That's until I began missing days at work and was fired. I don't think they ever knew about the food or the wine.

By mid 1977 I was in a worse state than I'd ever been. In fact, I was so bad that, once more, I ended up in the local mental hospital. The diagnosis was, psychiatric disorder due to alcoholic poisoning. After a few days in the hospital, without drink, I was a nervous wreck. I would sit and shake for hours at a time, sometimes rocking back and forth with my head between my hands. Terrified of my own thoughts, I often burst into floods of tears.

This condition was so unbearable that, after only a few days of drying out, I voluntarily signed myself out, just to get hold of a bottle of booze. As I reasoned it, the alcohol and drugs were keeping me alive. I couldn't live without them.

BOOZE, BOOZE, BOOZE

And that was just about true. I couldn't do anything without booze. Such mundane and routine matters as shaving, eating, and having a conversation had to be preceded with a drink. Otherwise, they were impossible.

I would do anything for drink. One night I was thrown out of a bar for pouring a glass of beer over a woman's head. Somewhat chastened I staggered outside and slumped down behind a bush. Hours later, when I awoke, it was pitch dark and the pub was deserted.

"The perfect opportunity for a free drink," I reasoned. Searching about for something suitable to help me break into the pub, I found a half-brick. It made a lovely hole in the window, just above the catch. Taking off my socks to use as gloves, I slipped the catch and was inside in a moment.

The cool pint of beer I pulled tasted sweet, and the fine King Edward cigar made lovely blue rings as its smoke curled towards the ceiling. "This is the life," I thought and, lying back in the chair with my feet on the table, contemplated how I might relieve this lonely pub of its stock.

The plan had only just begun to take shape in my mind when the place was suddenly bathed in light. Half a dozen policemen rushed in and formed a circle around me. "Caught red-handed this time John," the sergeant announced. "Looks like another spell in the Bar." He referred, I knew, not the pub I sat in, but to Barlinnie prison, in Glasgow.

A LIFE SAVER

Barlinnie it was. Really, it saved my life, for if I'd carried on the way I was going I'm sure I'd have been dead.

The usual hard, grim faces stared at me every day in Barlinnie. But I was changed. Rejected and dejected I shuffled around the exercise yard like an old man, wishing and hoping for death to come and release me from my misery.

On release from Barlinnie, Julie was waiting for me. The look in her eyes told me she was hoping, praying that it would be different this time. Back at the house I was surprised to find her sister there. Her name was Pat and she came from Glasgow.

There was a big carry-out meal in the centre of the floor and, on the stereo, Johnny Cash belted out "San Quentin I hate every inch of you ...." We lived in the top flat of a three story building, but the music could be heard all over the estate.

After the eats, and with Johnny still singing his heart out, I grabbed Pat and said "Come on, how about a dance?"

As I wheeled her around the floor Julie sang from the couch. Dancing is thirsty work so I went to the kitchen for a couple of beer glasses. What a shock was in store for me when I flung open the door. There stood a big Alsatian dog. I froze in my tracks.

"The dog's mine," Pat called in. "My man works on the oil rigs and the dog's good for protection. There's a lot of trouble up around where I live."

She assured me the dog was quite docile and, after feeding it a few scraps, I came to the same conclusion.

A MINI RIOT

After tea that night Pat was filling up the beer glasses again when the dog came bounding into the room. It made a bee line for my plate, lying on the floor, and cleaned up the scraps of food in an instant. I stretched out my hand to pat him on the pack, at which point he wheeled round and bit my thumb; drawing blood.

Screaming with the pain, and filled with violent anger, I brought my fist down on the dog's snout. Pat stood up to protest at my action and, with this, the dog jumped on my back, snarling and biting.

In desperation I grabbed the knife from where it lay on the floor and with a single thrust, stuck it into the dog's side.

Pat went wild with fury. She jumped at me, screaming in rage, pounding her fists on my back and yelling oaths and abuses at me. The dog attacked again, and again I struck with the knife, plunging it in three times in quick succession.

Now Julie was screaming, Pat was screaming, I was screaming, and the dog was barking, wailing and jumping up the walls in an effort to escape.

In the ensuing turmoil Julie opened a window and called out "Somebody help us" Please somebody, help us!"

Meanwhile I had struck Pat again, so savagely across the face that she went tottering backwards over a chair and finished up sprawled on the floor.

Leaping over the toppled chair I made for Julie, who was still at the window screeching for help. She was wearing a blouse. I grabbed the collar and tugged so violently that the buttons flew off and ricocheted off the walls and window pane.

By this time the dog was collapsed on the floor, licking its wounds.

BACK IN CLINK

There was a loud banging at the front door. Before I could stop her Julie ran and opened it. The police burst in to be confronted with a scene of devastation. Blood was spattered everywhere. There were broken ornaments, torn curtains, up-turned furniture and bleeding bodies. The first policeman to enter the living room stopped dead in his tracks at the sight he beheld. Another policeman walked towards me, knowing instinctively that I was the cause of the trouble. As he approached, I clenched my fist and drew it back in readiness to strike. That was one blow I never did strike. The policeman baton hit me sharply on the head and the familiar blackness descended.

When I came round I was on the way to the "meat wagon." The police had dragged me, unconscious, down the flights of stairs and now they led me, handcuffed and stumbling to their van.

Once inside, one of them turned to me and said "Do you know something, Wilson? I've seen some head-cases in my time in this job, but you are the most brutal, mad b_____ it's ever been my misfortune to come across."

I was in such a state, with blood seeping from the baton wound in the head that, for once, I kept my mouth shut. All I wanted was the solace of the police barrack cell, and some sleep.

Next morning, the police doctor patched me up, and in court the sheriff put me away again for four months. At the prison reception desk, the admissions officer looked up, and when he saw me he said dryly "Well John, back again?"

Chapter Nineteen

NICODEMUS AND ME

Later that evening, the key rattled in the lock and the warder swung open the cell door. Without a word he walked on to the next door and did the same. It was slop-out time on the first night of a new prison sentence.

Carefully, I carried the chamber pot to the sluice and emptied its contents. Turning round, a familiar face confronted me. It was Ron. I'd met him in prison before.

"O.K. Ron. How're you doin'?" I enquired.

"Just got three months, John. Another breach of the peace," he replied.

"I wonder where this peace is they keep talking about?" I asked, not really expecting an answer.

"God knows," moaned Ron. "It certain it's not for the likes of us."

"Oh well, maybe someday," I mused. "Maybe someday."

We nattered on for another minute or two and then the warden moved us on, back to our cells. I made a half-hearted attempt to read a spy novel, but slung it furiously against the wall in desperation. I just couldn't settle.

WHIRLPOOL

As on many occasions in the past, I buried my head in my hands and wrestled with my thoughts. My mind was like a whirlpool. Problems came at me from every direction and there was no way I could cope with them. Uppermost was the stark fact that, at twenty-seven years of age, here I was in prison again, starting my tenth sentence.

After years of searching for the true meaning of life (or so I told myself) I was no nearer to the answer. It seemed that the age old worldly philosophy of "the survival of the fittest" was the only thing that worked. Although, in my case, survival was about all it could be called.

On the way back from slopping out, when I grabbed the spy novel, I had also slipped a small New Testament into my pocket. I don't know why I was so secretive about wanting a Bible, but I suppose I'd didn't want any more ribbing from the other inmates.

A LESSON FROM NICODEMUS

I picked up the Testament and it fell open at the third chapter of John's gospel. The first fourteen verses, the account of Nicodemus coming to speak to Jesus, were enough for me. I lay back to think about them.

As far as I could make out, this man Nicodemus was a bit like me. He came to see Jesus at night because, obviously, he didn't want to be seen by his peers. In plain terms, he was ashamed. That was me, and that's why I had secretly brought the New Testament back to cell.

The more I thought about Nicodemus and his encounter with Jesus, the more I realised that, all those years ago, he had asked the very same question that I was now asking.

Three times, within the space of five verses, in John chapter three, Jesus had said to Nicodemus "Ye must be born again!" That's the message I'd heard in Bethany Hall, more than three years ago. And just as I was about to ask the question I'd asked so many times before, I realised that Nicodemus had asked it too. "How? How can a man be born again?"

"Nicodemus," I thought. "Nicodemus, a member of a devout religious sect. A man who knew the Bible from cover to cover. A man who prided himself in the strictness of his religious observance. And yet he didn't know anymore about the way to eternal life than a poor, hopeless drunkard. That, by itself, was something worth thinking about"

THAT HOW QUESTION

As I mused on all this, the night light went out and the cell was plunged into darkness. My eyes gradually became accustomed to the semi-darkness, and as they did, I reached out for my tobacco tin. Expertly rolling a smoke, I lit it and drew the first heavy draw, deep down into my lungs.

"Could I really be changed into another creature by the power of God's Spirit?" I wondered. From what I'd just read about Nicodemus it seemed possible. And yet I was still troubled by that "how" question. Would I ever find the answer? It took a long time for sleep to come that night.

"WAKEY, WAKEY!"

My slumber was abruptly ended by the voice of a prison officer singing "Wakey, wakey, rise and shine, empty those bladders of stale urine." The response of the inmates to this melodious wake up call was, as you might expect, rude in the extreme. They didn't appreciate the warden's sense of humour, and let him know it.

Later that day a few of us, including Ron, were transferred to Barlinnie Prison, in Glasgow. This was where I'd serve the remainder of my sentence.

A BIBLE PLEASE?

The thoughts about God were still with me, and so, in Barlinnie, I asked for a Bible. The prison officer to whom I made the request treated me with disdain. "Going religious are you Wilson?" he smirked. "Well God won't help you in this place boy. I'm the big boss in here." However, he put through my request.

A couple of days later, a minister appeared at the door of the laundry, where I was working. He was carrying a large black Bible. My stomach somersaulted.

"What will the guys think of this?" I wondered in alarm. And then another question came to mind, as if to rebuke me. "Are you ashamed of God?" Before I had time to think of the answer my name was called out, very loudly, by one of the guards.

Sheepishly, I made my way over to the desk, with every pair of eyes in that laundry burning a hole in the back of my head. The minister handed the Bible over, and then I had to make the long, lonely walk back to my job. What an experience! And what humiliating embarrassment!

BILLY GRAHAM?

A big lad from Glasgow, a real hard man, and nicknamed "The Beast" called out for all to hear. "Fancy yourself at the old Billy Graham caper then, John, eh?"

My response almost floored him. "What's wrong with reading the Bible then? It's a very interesting book, and anyway, who wants to read nonsense all the time?" The Beast just grunted.

A little later, I took some shirts into the sewing room and another Glasgow man tried to be smart. "Taking up the old Bible bashing game then, John?"

I dispatched with him in similar fashion. "Look pal, you might think it's some big joke, but I happen to believe in God. I believe in Heaven and Hell too. So get back to your sewing and mind your own business."

His face turned red with anger and he reached for a pair of scissors. To me, his intention was clear. But before his hand could reach their target, I crashed my foot into his shin and he doubled in two with pain. He apologised, and that was the end of the matter.

THE INNER BATTLE

Each night in my cell I read the Bible till the lights went out. Towards the end of my time in Barlinnie fear began to grip me. I didn't want to come back into a place like this, and yet I knew if a radical change didn't take place in my life, this was where I'd be. The drink would see to that.

On the morning of my release the real inner battle began. Part of me wanted to be right with God, part of me longed for the pleasures of sin. I knew which was the wiser route.

DESTITUTE

Back in Dumfries again, I had nowhere to live so began sleeping rough. To my mind, this justified getting a bottle of wine, and this in turn set me off on yet another drinking binge. For six months I slept in an old hotel in the centre of the town. Big Ron and I teamed up and became a pair of wild things. We begged, stole or threatened to get money and, most days, were successful.

The old hotel was infested with rats and, to avoid being nibbled at night, I slept in a cupboard with the door closed. Other tramps moved in along with us, so that the place became a den of thieves, alcoholics and vagabonds, with me as their leader.

Each week-day, one or other of the tramps was paid a Giro cheque by the social security services. This meant there was always money for booze. However, by Sunday, all the bottles were empty. For us, it was the worst day of the week. Burdened with self-pity, I sat in my cupboard all day, shaking and shivering for want of drink. I was so bad by this time that, on occasions I was reduced to drinking aftershave lotion.

In fact, about this time, an old prison mate of mine arrived in Dumfries, from London. His shock at seeing me at rock bottom so shook me that I quit drinking, almost overnight. Just at this time, too, my mother, whom I hadn't seen for years, met me in the street one day. She was so upset at seeing me in such an awful condition that she arranged a room for me. It was in this room that the whole course of my life was to change.

Chapter Twenty

GLORIOUS DELIVERANCE!

Early in 1979, I went back to the Bethany Hall and got in touch with the Christians there. In my heart I knew they were good people, full of kindness and understanding. There was just a chance they could help me.

Sammy was one of the first people I came into contact with there. He had a unique testimony. After doing a four year sentence for serious assault, he had drifted down to London where he became involved in the drug scene. Hooked on heroin, his health deteriorated to such an extent that, at one time, he was given only six months to live.

His girl-friend, at the time, was a back-sliden Christian. They got to talking about God and, wonderfully, she was restored - he was converted. Although this story moved me, even, in a way, encouraged me, I felt my crimes and misdeeds were too great to be forgiven.

I attended a few of the gospel meetings in Bethany Hall, but when nothing happened, went back to the drink. "God was unjust," I told myself. "Look how many starving refugees there are in the third world." What that had to do with me, a poor, drunken, down-and-out, I never took time to reason. It was just another excuse for my godless behaviour.

SUICIDE?

By now it was May 1979, and a few more criminal charges hung over my head. I'd managed to keep the room together, although I'd nearly been evicted a few times for getting behind with the rent.

By now, I was twenty-eighty years old, but I looked more like thirty-eight. Or so I was told. This situation couldn't go on any longer. But how would I end it?

I awoke one morning, feeling just as miserable as ever. There was only one solution to my problem. I would take the only way out - suicide. The window beckoned. At three stories up, it would be a quick death. Just as I was about to step up onto the sill to make the jump that would end it all, a single word slammed into my head - Jesus!

CONTRITION

Falling to my knees on the floor I cried out "God! You know what a sinner I've been. A drunkard, a thief, a blasphemer, a fornicator, a pervert, a no good violent man. You know I've done nothing good for anyone all my life. I've gone out of my way to harm your creations. Lord Jesus Christ will you save me? I confess now that I'm lost and need you to give me a new life. Will you come into my heart now and be my Saviour? If you do I'll serve you from this moment on."

Just then I felt a coolness all about me, like a gentle breeze. Inside, I felt completely different, so different that I began to cry. Floods of tears ran down my cheeks as I wept like a child. The more I wept, the greater the relief I felt. It was a wonderful, wonderful experience. It felt so real. It was so real. I knew in my heart that God had heard me. I knew he had saved me. I knew I'd never be the same again.

REPENTANCE

Drying my eyes, I looked around the room. There were pornography books, empty beer cans and wine bottles, pills, and a dozen other relics of my wild and debauched past. I gathered up the whole lot and chucked them into a carrier bag. Along with them I threw in my tobacco tin and cigarette lighter. Then I dumped the lot in the dust bin.

I could hardly believe the instant change that had taken place. There wasn't the least desire for drink, drugs, tobacco or any of the other things which, up till now, I hadn't been able to live without. In a moment, my whole personality had been changed and I felt completely different. Inside, I felt free - really free!

I often think about that little room. Although I wasn't aware of the physical presence of Jesus, I know that I met Him in person that day. It's something I'll never forget. Many a time since then I've sung a hymn that sums up my experience that wonderful day.

"In loving- kindness Jesus came,
my soul in mercy to reclaim,
and from the depths of sin and shame
through grace He lifted me.

"From sinking sand He lifted me;
with tender hand He lifted me;
from shades of night to plains of light,
O praise His name, He lifted me."

Later that evening, the window, through which I had planned to jump to my death, became a picture frame to me. From it, I had a lovely view of the river Nith, which runs through Dumfries. Although I'd lived in the town for most of my life, I hadn't been aware of the simple beauty of the place.

From the river, two swans took off in majestic flight. I stood watching them - transfixed. A man and woman passed by, with their two little girls. My heart went out to them, in admiration and affection. I'd never been like this before. My feelings towards nature and the world about me were such as I'd never known before, and it was amazing. Like another hymn writer again I could say .....

"Heaven above is softer blue,
earth below is sweeter green.
something lives in every hue,
Christless eyes have never seen.

Birds with gladder songs o'erflow,
flowers with deeper beauties shine,
since I know, as now I know,
I am His and He is mine."

CONFESSION

I couldn't wait until the next day. I wanted to tell someone what had happened to me. I went to see two Christian friends whom I knew would be pleased at the news of my conversion. They were delighted. "Praise the Lord, brother," were their first words, and then they prayed with me.

The following Sunday I was back at the Bethany Hall, telling the people there the good news that God had truly saved me. Right away they welcomed me with open arms and warm hearts. They had no hesitation in receiving me as a new brother in Christ.

Confessing Christ as my personal Saviour was the next thing I had to learn to do. This turned out to be more difficult than I had imagined, but it had to be done. Believing with the heart, confessing with the mouth - that's the rule, and I had to obey. At first it seemed easier to fight with someone than tell them that Jesus was now my Saviour. However, after about three months, most people who knew me had either heard the news directly from me, or had been told, on the grapevine, by somebody else.

THE ROARING LION

Of course, the Devil doesn't give up easily, and in my case he made sure there was plenty of temptation placed in my way. The Bible says that, "the Devil, as a roaring lion, walks up and down, seeking whom he may devour." I know the truth of that. In those first three months I was offered more drink and drugs than I'd seen in a long time. The "dope" was all at rock bottom prices too - very, very tempting. It didn't take me long to discover that Satan is ruthless, cunning and merciless in his pursuit of God's children. His purpose was to trap me if he could. Thankfully, the Lord, in His mercy, upheld me in these times of temptation and helped me to overcome the devil's wiles.

However, there were discouragements too. After a few weeks I moved into a bigger room, in the same building where my mum lived. By this time she and dad were divorced and, although she was happy to see me living a more sensible life, she couldn't see that it was God who had changed me. Whenever I spoke to her about my new found Saviour, she felt I was trying to persuade her to become religious. So it was discouraging not to be able to convince her that her real need was Jesus.

VICTORIES

Thankfully, the discouragements were outweighed by the victories. Six months after my own conversion I had the great joy, along with another Christian, of leading an ex-prison mate of mine to Jesus.

I'd not seen this man for a long time, so when we met, not knowing about my new life, he invited me into the pub for a drink. He was more than surprised when I told him "I've finished with all that stuff now John. I've found something a million times better - Jesus!

He thought I'd become a Mormon, or a Jehovah's Witness, or a member of some other exclusive sect. I related the story of how I'd come to know the Lord Jesus in a personal way, and of how he had transformed my life. I told him that the desire for drugs and drink and all the other things I'd lived for was now gone, and that life for me now was better than it had every been since I was born.

"John, I am IN Christ," I told him, "and it's absolutely wonderful!"

At the end of the conversation he shook my hand, thanked me, and said he would give it some thought. I was too young in the faith to believe anything other than that's what he would do, so I went home and prayed for him, asking God to give him the grace to believe in Jesus. Three weeks later, another friend and I knelt with him in prayer as he received Jesus into his heart. I wasn't at all surprised. Isn't that what God does? He answers prayer.

My mother was getting more interested in Jesus, too. She saw the change in my life and realised, eventually, that it wasn't something in me, it was the power of God. One evening, after returning from a gospel meeting she said "I'm ready to be saved now." What a thrill it was to have been instrumental in leading my own mother to the Lord.

Chapter Twenty-One

LEARNING TO LEAN

O ne night, about a year after my conversion, I'd been speaking at a youth rally. There was tea afterwards and one of the ladies gave me a box of sandwiches that had been left over. Walking home, at about 10.45pm on a Saturday night in the pouring rain, I noticed a man standing by the roadside, hitching a lift. He was carrying a small suitcase.

Understanding how he felt, I walked over to him and offered the sandwiches. "I hope you won't be offended," I added. He looked at me with relief. "I've just now been praying that God would provide for my hunger," he replied, then added "I'm a born again Christian."

Gripping his hand in a firm handshake I asked if he wanted a place to stay, adding "I'm a Christian too." Back at my room, after he had a shower and we had a meal together, Tom told me his story.

"Eleven years ago, John, I was a wealthy businessman, in Ireland. Every evening, a friend and I went to a hotel, dined on the very best of food and then got ourselves drunk on whiskey. I owned a powerful Jaguar car and one night on the way home we crashed into a field at 70 miles an hour. I ended up sitting in the field in the driving position, my friend was twenty yards away screaming to death in the burning car. At that moment I received Jesus Christ as my Saviour.

He went on to tell me that, after this, he sold his business, bought a smaller house, and devoted his time to preaching the gospel all over the country. His ministry brought him into contact with many of the men involved in illegal organisations. Some of these men came to know the Lord through his witness and, as a consequence, left those organisations.

GODFATHERS

This upset the godfathers, who visited their wrath on the man responsible. They picked him up, drove him to his house, and gave him five minutes to gather together a few essential belongings. Then they petrol bombed his home and banished him from Ireland.

Tom opened the suitcase. It was full of gospel tracts. "This is all I could rescue, John. Praise Jesus!" After prayer together, for the oppressed and the oppressors in Ireland, we retired for the night.

Next morning, Sunday, I walked him down the road to the spot where we had met. With the mutual promise to each other of prayer, we said goodbye.

THE PREACHER

From the beginning of my Christian life I couldn't contain my desire to spread the gospel. Open air meetings suit me best. I've had the privilege of speaking at hundreds of open air services all over the country, and very rarely are they dull occasions.

Once, at a service in my home town, Dumfries, a man ran towards me uttering oaths and curses. My initial instinct was to call on some of my old street skills, and fell him. However, common sense and the influence of the Holy Spirit prevailed. Even though he tried to kick the daylights out of me, I truly felt compassion for him.

By the time the police arrived to take him away, a large crowd had gathered to see what the fuss was about. I didn't miss the opportunity to preach Christ to them. When the police called about a week later, inviting me to press charges against the man who had disturbed the meeting, I told them to forget it. "But he would have had you sent to prison if the boot had been on the other foot," they protested. "I know, I know," I replied, "but sending that poor creature to prison won't do him any good. Only Jesus can help him."

WEDDING BELLS

After a courtship of eight months Carole, my girlfriend, and I decided to marry. Most people we knew, Christians and non Christians approved of the match and wished us well, but there were a few who thought it unwise. Why, I'm not really sure. Perhaps they still had little faith in me. Perhaps they still thought I'd lapse back to my old ways, sooner or later. However, God had said of me, as of every other born again believer "Old things are passed away, behold all things are become new." Carole and I felt our decision to marry was in accordance with the will of God. To us, that's all the mattered, and I believe time has proved us right.

However, even marriage wasn't without incident, in the early days. One night, my old friend Ron, with whom I'd teamed up after my last release from prison, came round to our house. Carole and I were sitting quietly at home when there was a loud banging at the front door. When I open it, there stood big Ron, swaying from side to side, obviously drunk.

"Give me a pair of boots," he demanded. I didn't have any boots, and I told him so, asking him to leave lest he upset Carole.

SOME CHRISTIAN!

"Call yourself a Christian!" he roared. "You're nothing but fake!" (Actually, he said much worse than this but I daren't print it.) At this, I realised that reasoning with Ron was out of the question, so I slammed the door and slid the bolt into place. In an instant, a fist came through one of the small panes in the door, showering broken glass all over me and the floor. The other five panes followed in quick succession. By this time Carole was screaming hysterically and I was doing my best to hold the door against Ron's efforts to shoulder it in.

Carole grabbed the phone and began dialling 999, but before she could finish I called to her not to bother because Ron seemed to have given up. All went quiet and I took Carole in my arms to comfort her.

As she wiped away the tears and I did my best to calm her, Ron appeared again, this time at the window of the living room. His hands were dripping with blood and he was bellowing abuse and threats. Almost before we could take in the gravity of this new situation he stuck his fist through this window too. Pane after pane followed in quick succession.

There was pandemonium as fragments of glass flew everywhere across the living room. This time Carole did phone the police and waited till they answered. By now, Ron was at the door again, shouldering it with all his drunken might. With one final heave the bolt gave way and the door slammed against the inner wall. There stood Ron, like a raging bear, threatening to kill me.

I'LL KILL YOU!

A carving knife lay on the table and my first reaction was to plunge it into his chest. However, common sense prevailed and I thought better of it. Ron was not so sensibly, or kindly disposed. He grabbed my throat and was making a very good job of choking me, while at the same time, calling me vile and filthy names.

With Carole still screaming hysterically, Ron tightened his grip on my throat and threatened to kill me. Helpless to overcome his enormous strength I croaked "Killing me won't make God go away Ron. Jesus died for the ungodly!" To my surprise, at this he let go and fell to his knees sobbing and crying out "I'm sorry, I'm sorry!" That's where he was when the police arrived and took him away. As they led him down the path he was still crying and called back to me "I want Jesus too, John."

MY DAD

By this time my mum and dad were divorced about two years. It's a great source of regret to me that I never got to love them and be with them as a family. By the time the Lord saved me they were already separated. Now that I was a Christian, my love for them increased and deepened. It was too late to bring them together again, but surely not to late to witness to them and to see them brought into God's family. My mother had already come to know the Lord, as I've explained, but my dad was still far from the kingdom. I felt it my duty to try and win him for the Saviour.

When I first went to see him, after I was saved, he was very dismissive of what had taken place in my life. "So you've got religion, have you?" His tone was almost sarcastic. "Good, I hope it does you some good. You need that sort of thing. You can't handle life on your own. As for me, I'll be all right on the day."

"Dad, you won't be all right," I remonstrated with him. "If you die without Christ, you'll die in your sins. There'll be no hope for you. Only Jesus can set you free. Only He can free you from the guilt and penalty of sin."

At first he wouldn't listen to anything I said. However, after a time he was a bit more responsive and allowed me to leave him a New Testament, and some tracts. I had high hopes that he would give some thought to what I had said, realise that there was a change in me, and perhaps read the tracts, at least. A few days after we met, however, the Bible and tracts were returned with a note saying he didn't want to see me ever again. For me, that was heart breaking.

Chapter Twenty-Two

REACHING OUT

My witness for Christ began taking me all over the country. I was willing to go anywhere to speak for the one who had changed my life. Sometimes, the most amazing things happened. They still do!

The railway station in Birmingham is a busy place, with crowds of people coming and going all day long. It's a great place to hand out gospel tracts. Many refuse them, but there's always plenty who accept.

I was standing there one day, handing out tracts to the passers by, when an old man walked up to me and muttered "Are you going to the Birmingham City Mission?" Then, just as quickly as he had appeared, he melted back into the crowd and was gone.

"The Birmingham City Mission? What can he mean," I thought. When I'd finished tracting I asked a porter if he knew where the mission was. He did, and following his directions, I walked down the road and found it, just opposite the Ice Rink.

Peering through a window I could see between 40 and 50 men, rough looking in appearance, sitting talking. Down and outs, and winos, I realised. Through the next window I could see three men working in a kitchen. One of them, wearing a woolly hat, stirred at a large pot of soup.

HALLELUJAH BROTHER!

Slipping in through a side door I approached the man in the woolly hat. Almost apologetically I stammered "I don't really know why I'm here ... I'm a born again Christian ....." Before I could finish the sentence, he boomed "Hallelujah Brother," pumping my hand up and down in greeting. Then he elaborated.

"Less than an hour ago I was praying for someone to come and speak to these men. This is the first time in five years I've not had a message ready for them. It's great you've come. It's a real answer to prayer."

Vic was his name, and he ran the place. I gave them a hand to distribute the food to the men and then gave them my testimony. There was a great hush over the place as I spoke. The men listened very attentively. I suppose most of them could relate to what I said. Afterwards, I spoke to many of them personally, and as I did my heart went out to them. I thought "There, but for the grace of God go I."

PURPOSE.

At last, I was beginning to feel there was a purpose to life. In the past I'd often been troubled by questions about life. Where did I come from? What was I doing here? And, where was I going? But now that I'd come to know Jesus as Saviour, these questions no longer troubled me. I'd found life's purpose now - it was to serve Jesus.

The Birmingham experience had taught me to follow the leading of God. It taught me, too, that God often leads in the most simple and ordinary ways. I was determined to follow Him wherever He would lead.

Alistair, a friend and brother in the Lord, from Dumbarton, asked me if I'd like to attend the Greenbelt Christian Music Festival, held annually in England. Over the years I've been to three or four of these events and have had the pleasure of sharing the platform with such celebrities as Cliff Richard, Roy Castle, Fred Lemon, Larry Norman, John Stott and Garth Hewitt.

Christians, I found, were quite different to every other class of people I'd met. Even the most famous of them, the big names, were just humble vessels of the Lord, serving Him from their hearts, and doing His will. I have to say, they were all very kind to me and gave me great encouragement in everything I did.

GREENBELT

Greenbelt was a great learning experience for me and one I'd thoroughly recommend to all young Christians. At one of their festivals I met three wonderful Americans. Two were in the American Air Force and were based at Ipswich. The other was over to do a thing called "Banner Outreach." Bob Bible was his name. "Very appropriate," I thought. He was a travelling evangelist and had come to Britain to help spread the Word of God.

Bob and I became immediate friends and very soon teamed up to work together. We'd go out into the surrounding towns and villages, giving out tracts and preaching the gospel. It was a great learning experience for me.

Eventually, Bob came back with me to Dumfries. It must have been a strange sight for the people of my home town, and of Dumfries and Galloway district, to see a half cripple helping to carry a religious banner through the streets and along the roads. One side of the banner proclaimed "Ye must be born again!" The other, "By grace are ye saved!"

I refer to my self as a half cripple. To explain this you have to remember that I was still suffering the consequences of that car accident all those years ago. My feet, which had been damaged beyond repair, will never heal completely. It's something I'll have to live with till the end of my days. I've lost count of the number of times I wish I could turn the clock back to that night on Christmas eve 1967, when I joined my mate for a joy ride to Carlisle in the gas van. However, I've learned that, although God forgives our sins, we often have to live with the consequences of them. Still, He gives grace for each day.

Bob Bible and I took that banner to nearby towns like Moffat, Lockerbie, Castle Douglas and Dalbeattie. We held it high all over the west of Scotland. And then we did the big cities like Edinburgh, Glasgow, Carlisle and Newcastle. We also witnessed in many other smaller places along the way.

OLYMPIC INVITATION

Eventually, Bob had to go back to America, to California, but before he left he invited me to join him in Los Angeles for the 1984 Olympic Games. All I had to do was get the air-fare. He would take care of the rest.

I've learned since then that God always finances His will, and obviously I wanted to go. But where would I get the money for a flight to California? This would need much prayer.

Around April 1984, I was invited to conduct the Easter meetings at Netherhall Christian Hotel, Largs, Scotland. John Allison, who ran the meetings, invited myself, my wife Carole, and our daughter Rebekah to spend the week-end at the hotel. In return I would speak at all the meetings.

On the Friday night over a hundred people gathered in the large lounge to hear my testimony. At the end a woman came and handed me a small brown envelope saying "The Lord has told me to give this to you. You will know what to do with it."

GOD PROVIDES

As we retired to bed that night I opened the envelope and drew out a cheque for five hundred pounds. Carole and I bowed our heads and thanked God for answering our prayers. The trip to the Olympic games was on.

About a month before leaving for the U.S.A. the two brothers from the American Air Base called me with an invitation to speak at the base. It was a wonderful time of witness and fellowship, with over a hundred and thirty people gathering to hear me.

On the Saturday afternoon a group of us went into Ipswich town to witness in the open air. I sent the two brothers to each end of a shopping arcade to give out tracts, while I stayed in the middle to preach the gospel.

TROUBLE

After just five minutes a crowd of young "punk" type youths surrounded me. There must have been about forty of them. I continued the preaching, holding forth against drink, drugs and the dangers of addiction. The first blow hit me on the back of the head and I went down like a sack of flour. My Bible was torn from my hand and then they got stuck in with the feet. All I could do was to roll into a ball and wait for the kicking to stop. They eventually scattered when the sound of a police siren was heard. By this time my friends had been alerted by the commotion and ran to my aid.

The outcome of all this was that local Christians in Ipswich realised how little they had been doing to witness for Christ publicly. Soon after that, three separate groups of Christians got involved in spreading the good news of salvation in their own town.

Chapter Twenty-Three

OLYMPIC GOLD

I n July 1984 I hugged and kissed Carole and Rebekah goodbye and left for five weeks in California, at the Olympic Games. To say that I travelled light is an understatement. All I had with me, apart from what I wore, was one change of clothes and two bags of tracts.

As I flew over the great, sprawling metropolis of Los Angeles, the realisation of how small I was hit me. I felt so insignificant, coming to this great city and to these historic games. Yet I believed that it was God purpose that I should be here. The words of George Hoffman came to mind "One person cannot change the world, but you can change the world for one person." This was all I wanted - to help, in some small way, to change the world of some poor, struggling fellow human being.

Outside the airport there were about fifty people gathered to welcome me. This gave a tremendous emotional boost. And amongst the crowd, the one face I recognised, that of Bob Bible.

SAN FRANCISCO

Next day, Bob and I set out on the long drive to San Francisco, where the Democratic Convention was being held. There would be crowds of people there - a good place to distribute gospel tracts.

On arrival at the Berkley University Campus we set up the banner and began witnessing to the thousands of students who were out for lunch. We spent about an hour preaching, handing out tracts and speaking, one to one, to the students. A couple of young girls came up to us and proffered glasses of iced water. In the hot sun of California nothing could have been more welcome.

One of the girls handed me a cheque. It was for $150. "It's from that man over there," she said, pointing to a gentleman who wore a hearing aid. "Is he deaf?" I asked. "Yes!" she said. "And dumb too!" "How did he know what I was saying?" I enquired. "You'd better ask him that yourself," she advised. "Look, he insists you take the money, so why don't you just accept it and be thankful." That was good advice, I thought and so, pocketing the cheque, I thanked the man and we left the University.

UNION PARK

Driving the big camper trailer into the centre of town we headed for Union Park and searched for somewhere to park. A quick telegram to Heaven got an equally quick response. We spotted an R.V. Centre, that's a special park for camping vehicles, and drove in. "It'll cost you $150 for ten days," said the car park attendant. "Will you take this cheque," I asked, and handed him the cheque I'd been given just a short time ago. After a quick inspection the man said "No problem!" Our parking problems were solved, with the bill paid. As Bob manoeuvred the camper into position I thought on the words of Scripture "Before you call I will answer!"

Next day we ventured up to Union Square, in the middle of San Francisco, where thousands of people were gathered for a big Gay Rights rally.

"GLAD TO BE GAY!" - "GAY IS GOOD!" - and "GOD LOVES GAYS!" their banners proclaimed. On a rough raised platform a figure, dressed as a nun, with full habit, rosary beads and heavy make up, prepared to address the crowd. He was Sister Boom Boom, the political spokesman for the San Franciso homosexual population. As he spoke the vast crowd chanted and roared their approval of every word their leader uttered.

Bob and I manoeuvred our way into the middle of this crowd and raised a banner with a scripture text on it. We also wore tee shirts which proclaimed "JESUS SAVES FROM HELL!"   On reflection, this probably wasn't one of the safest, or sanest things I'd ever been involved in. The crowd didn't like our presence there, and they didn't like the message we had for them.

VIOLENCE!

As I stood there, gripping the banner with one hand and giving out tracts with the other, the crowd advanced toward me. Next moment I was on the ground, holding my head between my hands. My eyes were burning in their sockets and a confusion of thoughts raced through my head.

"What kind of a God would bring you half way across the world to have you attacked by a thug and blinded?" My eyes were burning even more fiercely. I couldn't see a thing. I could hear voices - shouting, laughing, mocking, screaming. But I hardly knew whether they for shouting for me or against me. A voice cut through the din. "You'll be all right! Someone has sprayed Mace in your eyes. It's stuff the police use to disarm unruly people and criminals. Sometimes old ladies and even younger women get it on prescription from the doctor, to protect them on subways at night. It'll wear off soon and the blindness will go."

Bob helped me to my feet and dusted me down. Two young Christian girls appeared, as from nowhere, and began bathing my eyes with cold water. They, too, reassured me that I'd be all right.

We were still surrounded by homosexuals, shouting abuse and threatening further violence. Eventually, a couple of police officers arrived on the scene. They were sympathetic to our situation, but thought we'd been a bit imprudent to do what we did in the middle of a crowd so hostile to the gospel.

That night, by which time my sight had returned to normal, we gave thanks to God for sparing us in the tribulations of that day. "Blessed are ye when men shall revile you for my sake," we thought, and praised God for being counted worthy to suffer abuse for His name.

THE PARADE

A much larger parade was planned for next day. About a hundred thousand homosexuals were expected to march right through the centre of the city, to flaunt their wicked purposes before all. We had our plans too. Four other Christian brothers had agreed to meet us at a pre-determined place and to help us with outreach and witness at the big parade.

As we met and began putting our plans into operation a carnival atmosphere was developing in the parade. Thousands of homosexuals swanned about arm in arm - men with men, women with women. They were drinking, smoking dope, dancing, singing, and generally going wild. As well as the crowds who walked, there were truck loads of others, many of them dressed in clothes of the opposite sex. To me, it was a most offensive scene.

FLAK JACKETS

One of the men who joined us to help with the witness was Jeremiah, the 1983 arm wrestling world champion. He opened a large bag and, groping inside, began to pull out the contents, saying at the same time "I didn't bring one for you John!" "One what?" I enquired. "A bullet-proof jacket," he replied, quite calmly. "It's not unusual for a crowd of this type to take a few shots at us, you know." "Great!" I thought. "Here we are, six Christians in the middle of a hundred thousand homosexuals, and now someone tells me there's a chance of being shot! What next?"

A large banner had been made ready, with scripture verses and the words "NO NO HOMO!" emblazoned on it. Since I was the only one without a flak-jacket, it was decided I would carry the banner. That doesn't sound as illogical as it seems. The plan was that I would hold the banner aloft and the other five would stand in front of me, wearing their flak-jackets, as a kind of human shield. At the same time they gave out gospel tracts and called out verses from the Bible to those who passed by.

We did not go un-noticed. As the crowds filed slowly past our little group they hurled verbal abuse at us, threw Coke bottles (some of them full) beer cans, coins and batteries. Some of them found their mark, but we stood our ground till almost all of the parade had passed by.

TATTOO

By this time we were all exhausted. I had been holding the banner aloft for hours and the sleeve of my tee shirt had gradually crept up my arm till it was almost at my shoulder. This revealed a tattoo from years ago. It said Jim & John. It was something I'd had done years ago as a friendship sign to an old pal of mine. However, when the homosexuals of San Francisco saw it they suspected the obvious and cried out "Look! He's one of us."

Instead of being friendly towards me, they were even more angry and began pulling at the banner and shouting abuse at me. I suppose they looked upon me as a traitor to their cause. Thankfully, at that point, the mounted police arrived and surrounded us. I don't think I have ever been so glad to see the strong arm of the law. They did a superb job, protecting us and scattering the crowd which fled in all directions.

ERASING THE PAST

On the way back to the trailer camp I asked Bob to let me off at a tattooist. "Come back in a couple of hours," I said. When he did the old tattoo had been replaced by a new one - a rose with a cross and the words "Jesus Saves!" "There'll be no more abuse from the Devil about Jim and John," I told Bob. "Old things are passed away, behold all things are become new."

I should say that I don't believe Christians should have tattoos on their bodies. I think it's unscriptural. However, if you already have one I can see no harm in changing it, as I did, as a witness for Christ.

The five weeks in America was wonderful and a great learning experience. Everyday was an adventure of faith. We gave out thousands of tracts, witnessed personally to hundreds of people and planted the precious seed of the Word of God in many hearts.

WAR & PEACE

There were tough times and good times. I was beaten up three times, threatened with a shotgun, sprayed in the eyes, spat on, cursed and badmouthed. But even in the midst of all these trials there were funny moments. Once, at a "Legalise Marijuana," protest, I was lying curled up on the ground being kicked by a few of the demonstrators. Out of the corner of my eye I managed to get a glimpse of the tee shirt worn by one of my attackers. "Peace!" it said.

But against that, I remember a wonderful occasion at a football stadium when a hundred and twenty thousand Christians joined together in the singing of "Amazing grace." What a thrill!

Chapter Twenty-Four

HOME AGAIN

B ack home in Dumfries I suddenly realised how fortunate and blessed I was to live in such a beautiful place. Growing up, I had never liked my home town. In fact, I hated it. That was probably because I had been guilty of so much wrong there. But now my attitude was changing. This little Scottish town was my home, and now I loved it.

It may be, it is a lovely little town, but it has many people who need the gospel. Once, I was standing outside Woolworths, in Dumfries, handing out tracts. The banner I carried said on one side "THE WAGES OF SIN IS DEATH!" and on the other "THE GIFT OF GOD IS ETERNAL LIFE!" Two well-to-do ladies walked up to me and asked what this was all about. I explained that the statements on the banner were quotations from the Bible. "What's the wages of sin?" one of them roared. "The wages of sin, madam, is the payment due to everyone who refuses the free gift of eternal life through the finished work of the Lord Jesus Christ," I replied.

ABUSE & INSULTS

At this, both women launched into a barrage of abuse and insults. The air was blue with their oaths and curses. The venom and invective directed against the gospel even stunned an old campaigner like me.

It turned out they were lesbians and, I suppose, secretly, they knew that the Bible condemned their relationship. "We are both in love with each other," they screamed. "What's wrong with that? Surely God tells us to love one another, doesn't He?"

I explained how the love that God spoke of had to be pure love, not love as the world knew it, which is little better than lust. And certainly not the so called love of the Homo-sexual. In God's eyes that is corrupt, impure, wicked and an abomination in His sight.

SPITTING

This message was not what they wanted to hear. One of them spat full in my face. Then they both stormed off, hand in hand, into Woolworths. How strange, I often think to myself, that those who profess love, and talk so much about love, have absolutely no love, not even any tolerance, for those who disagree with them. What hope would there be, I wonder, if such people had control of power or government? There would be little liberality shown to those who profess Christ as Saviour and who desired to proclaim His gospel.

Fortunately, the Lord gave me grace not to react angrily to the abuse and insults of the two women outside Woolworths. It was a good job. A few days later, a man who had known me for years, even in my unsaved days, met me in the street. He knew I was now a professing Christian and, perhaps, he had been keeping an eye on me from a distance.

Anyway, he stopped me in the street and said "If ever I needed proof that there has been a genuine change in your life, John, that recent incident outside Woolies provided it." I suppose he realised that if such a scene had taken place in my unregenerate days, I'd have left the pair of them almost for dead.

"Well," I said, "The grace of God is a wonderful thing, and it makes a marvellous change in a man's life. When things like the incident outside Woolworths happen to me now, I count them as much an encouragement as if someone shouted words of praise at me."

ENCOURAGEMENT

When I think of encouragement it's impossible to escape the help given to me by many Christian friends along the way. Perhaps chief amongst these were Sam and Anna. Sam was, in many ways, the ideal person to help me. He was a former heroin addict and gang leader who had served time, as a young offender, for violence.

On release, he went to London and soon got involved in the new "Hippie," scene that was sweeping the world. Marijuana was becoming popular. It was top of the drug parade and under its influence thousands of young people were "turning on, tuning in and dropping out."

Anna came from a God fearing family. She was a backslidden Christian and went down to London expressly to get into the Hippie scene. Sam and Anna met in one of the Hippie "squats," as they were called, fell in love and became partners.

At one time, Sam's drug addiction was so bad that the doctors gave him only six months to live. However, even in the midst of their rebellion against the Almighty, He had a plan for them and it would be fulfilled.

THE JUKE BOX

Even though he wasn't a Christian, Sam was seeking for answers. One day, in a pub, as they talked about God, he said to Anna, "If the next record to come on the juke box is a hymn, I'll accept Jesus as my saviour. The juke box crackled into life and, to their astonishment, began to play "Rock of Ages." Stunned by what they heard they tried to explain it away as coincidence.

"If the next record is also a hymn, I'll definitely accept Jesus," said Sam, quite convinced he wouldn't have to fulfil his promise. The juke box dropped the needle on the next record and began to play "Amazing Grace."

THE PRIEST

They left the pub and headed for Dumfries. Sam had some contacts there. They went to a Catholic priest and asked him if he could tell them how to be saved. He didn't know, said he had never understood the term, but directed them to a local lady who was a born again Christian.

Mrs. Aston knew exactly what to do and what to say. She made them both welcome and after a few hours instruction led Sam to the Lord.

Anna was restored to her former faith and trust in Jesus. What a wonderful day for them both, and for Mrs. Aston.

That was 1977, and ever since then Sam and Anna have devoted themselves to the service of the Lord. They were a great help to me in my early days as a Christian. Twenty years on and they are still helping young believers to find their feet on the pathway of faith.

LIVING FOR JESUS

Help was what I needed. Now that I was a Christian I wanted to live for Jesus, just as avidly as I'd lived for my former master, Satan. Why shouldn't I? I'd given the Devil all of my life, thus far, and he hadn't paid me very well. I'd lost the proper use of my legs. I was minus a kidney. I'd spent years locked up behind the iron bars of prisons all over the country, and for most of that time I'd been little better than a down and out. Serving Jesus could only be better.

It has turned out that I'm in a very good position to be of service to the King of Kings. I've found out, too, that God has a place in His kingdom of service for everyone who wants to serve. I've never been to Bible school. My education is little improved from when I left school at sixteen. However, that in no way prevents me from speaking to sinners for Christ. In fact, it's very often an advantage. Many times, because of my background and my first hand understanding of the problems suffered by people from my side of the tracks, I can relate to them better than anybody else.

That's not to disparage education, or Bible Colleges, or the ordained ministry. Far from it. I have the greatest respect for those who have set aside two or three years of their lives to devote themselves to Bible studies. It's obvious that the better equipped you are the more prepared you are for every eventuality. But the hard school of experience is a good teacher too, and prepares you for situations that Bible College never does. However, each has its place, and the two can, and should, work together in harmony for the extension of the Kingdom.

HAPPY IN GOD'S WILL

However, I'm happy with my situation. I believe it's where the Lord wants me to be. Certainly, I've been able to help a lot of people in my years as a Christian. Once after a gospel meeting, where I had given my testimony, a man approached me. He confided to me that his whole life had been lived in fear and anger. He still had terrible bouts of anger from time to time. Much that I had spoken of he had been able to identify with, but how could he get rid of this obsessive anger? All I could do was to give him a more in-depth account of my own struggle and hope that this would be used by the Lord to help him. It was. That man is now a great open-air worker and has helped me with my witness on numerous occasions.

Anger is something that besets many people in our society. But it can be overcome by the grace of God. A couple of times recently I was invited on to the television programmes "KILROY," and "THE TIME, THE PLACE." On both programmes I was given the opportunity, albeit briefly, to explain the anger which had filled my heart for years, and how the Lord had delivered me from it.

I said that for years I had harboured a hatred for figures of authority, especially policemen, judges and prison officers. These people, it seemed at that time to me, were depriving me of the lifestyle I wanted to live. They were collectively preventing me from doing the things I wanted to do. I hated them for that and was constantly angry with them.

However, I realise now that the people I hated were just ordinary souls doing a day's work. What they did, or had to do in the line of duty, was not particularly directed against me, it was their job, and I shouldn't have been angry with them for doing it. Thankfully, I see things differently now.

Chapter Twenty-Five

WHO'S WHO

O ne night, a few years ago, as I watched "Rumpole of the Bailey," something caught my eye. It was a large red volume in the book-case behind where the actor, Leo McKern, was sitting. It was so big that I could make out the printing on the spine, quite clearly. "Who's Who," I called to my wife. "What's that book, Who's Who?" Carole explained that it was a compilation of all the famous and important people in the land. I had an idea. What if I wrote to as many of them as possible, sending them a copy of my testimony? The more I thought about it, the more I liked the idea.

In due course I got a copy of "Who's Who," and began my task. Along with the testimony I sent a brief note, which explained who I was and requested a signed photograph, if that wasn't too much trouble. The response has been amazing. Over the years I've compiled several albums of photographs and letters from hundreds of well known people. The list includes Bob Hope, Olivia De Haviland, Oliver Reed, Sir Anthony Hopkins, Bobby Charlton, Henry Cooper, Ted Dexter, Michael Heseltine, Glenda Jackson, Cleo Laine, Johnny Dankworth, Rita Tushingham, Susan Hampshire, Dr. Christian Barnard, Ian Holm, Twiggy, Charlton Heston, Ken Dodd, Norman Wisdom, Deborah Kerr, Bob Hoskins, Andrew Lloyd Webber, Sir Stanley Matthews, Tom Finney, Barbara Castle, Bob Dylan, Bishop Desmond Tutu, David Attenburgh,

Ronnie Barker, John Hurt, Ludovic Kennedy, Bryan Forbes, Christopher Lee, and the man who sort of gave me the idea and started the ball rolling, Leo McKern.

It's been a source of great joy to me to be an ambassador of Jesus to all these famous people.

FOOTBALL

Another area where I've found great opportunities for witness is in sport, especially football. As a child I had been crazy about soccer, playing it at every opportunity. My heroes were Ralph Brand, Joe Baker, Bobby Collins, Bobby Charlton, Jimmy Greaves, Dennis Law, George Best and Jim Baxter. On the football field I imagined myself turning into one of these characters and, someday, emulating them on the sacred turf of Wembley.

My accident put paid to all those dreams and ended even the possibility of a friendly game of football now and again. I became very bitter, to the point of loathing the sport. However, a few years ago, my daughter Rebekah developed an interest in soccer. We began watching the games on television and the old passion was re-kindled. It struck me that here was another opportunity to witness for Jesus.

I began with the local games, going along to a prominent spot, setting up the gospel banner and handing out tracts to the masses that filed in to watched their heroes do battle. It was a good training ground. Standing in a big, strange city, where nobody knows you is one thing, and in a sense, relatively easy. Standing at the football ground in your home town, where thousands know you, is quite different. Many an insult was hurled at me, and on a few occasions there were fists and feet used to attack me. Having said that, I have to report that nearly all witness in the open-air goes off without incident. It's only on very rare occasions that people give me any trouble. Still, you never know when the trouble is going to come, so you have to be on your toes all the time.

The experiences in my home town gave me the courage to extend the witness farther afield. I've already told you about the Olympic Games, in Los Angeles. Since then I've displayed the gospel banner at the Wimbeldon Tennis Championships, and given out tracts at Wembley Cup Finals, Premier League matches, minor matches all over the country and, more recently, some of the European Football Championship games in 1996.

THE BANNERMAN

My banner has been seen on television many times and I've had a lot of coverage in the national press too. I've been referred to as "The Strange Bannerman," and "The Alarming Man from Scotland with the Jesus Saves Tee Shirt."

It's always a great thrill to me when the Lord gives me what I call the "go-ahead." for a job. I pack the banner and the bag full of tracts, kiss my wife and daughter good-bye and head off for the station. Sitting on the train I feel almost like a soldier going to the front line. And I suppose, in a way, I am.

Two nights before the English/Scottish clash at Wembley, in the 1996 European Football Championships, I got to thinking about the best way to go about witnessing there. A story from the life of the missionary, Hudson Taylor, came to me. The great man had been in China for many years, and yet had never seen anyone converted to Christianity. The thought struck him that it was time to change tactics. He decided to discard his western clothing and adopt the garb of the local people. The result was dramatic and immediate. From that day his missionary endeavours prospered.

TARTAN ARMY

Thinking about this, and the great Tartan Army that would be at Wembley, I decided that, I too, should dress for the part. What I needed was a Scottish Football top. But where would it come from? I couldn't afford the £40 to buy one. The night before the match a young lad from across the way came to my door. What was he holding but the very shirt I needed. He gave it to me for £2.

At the match, I stood between the famous twin towers of Wembley and surveyed the spectacle. It was breathtaking. Thousands of wonderful colourful souls cheering and shouting for Scotland - and at the same time, staring at my banner with the words "YE MUST BE BORN AGAIN," and "BY GRACE ARE YE SAVED!"

Afterwards, I spoke to hundreds of supporters and took names and addresses to send books and tapes to.

When I first began the banner and tract witness it was pretty tough life. I didn't have the money for Bed & Breakfast accommodation so had to sleep rough. Bus shelters, park huts, railway stations and old garages were where I stayed. Many a morning I awoke as stiff as a board, cold and damp. However, over the years, through meeting many Christian friends, I've built up a list of people all over the country who willingly put me up for a night or two. All I have to do now is pick up the phone, ring one of these friends and my accommodation at base is arranged.

BACK IN THE JAILS!

Being led into prison work was no great surprise to me. You could probably say that an ex-jailbird like me, now delivered by God's grace, is the ideal person to help those still behind bars. Working with the Prison Fellowship, all over the world, has been a delight and a blessing far beyond my expectation. Big Colin Cuthbert, who helps to run the Scottish Prison Fellowship, has been used of God to get me into many prisons. That sounds a bit odd, doesn't it? I never had a problem getting into jail in my ungodly days. But now that I've paid my debt to society and no longer deserve to be behind bars, it can be really difficult to get into prison to visit the men there.

Just recently Colin Cuthbert and I did a tour of Scottish prisons. To me, as you can imagine, there's just something especially thrilling and wonderful about taking the gospel into prison. And you can imagine what it meant to me to walk into Barlinnie again, for the first time, with the gospel.

FLASH BACK

When I stepped through those great gates again, and stared into the faces of the men there, all I could see was my own reflection. In the faces of those men I saw the pain, the anger, the fear and the bitterness that plagued me for so long. But now I know that all those old fears and pains can be washed away - by faith in Christ Jesus.

Many a time I've stood, almost goggle eyed, at the sight of a group of saved prisoners singing, clapping and, sometimes, even dancing to the choruses of the Christian praise books. In situations like that I realise the truth of the old saying "Walls and bars do not a prison make."

There are many fine Christians in prison and a good number of them are using their time there to spread the good news of the gospel. With others, they are trying to make poor benighted souls realise that there's truth in the old lines ....

"Two men look through prison bars,
One sees mud, the other stars!"

But more important than that, they are following the advice of Jesus outlined in Matthew's Gospel, Chapter 25 ....

"I was hungry, and you gave me meat: I was thirsty, and you gave me drink: I was a stranger, and you took me in: naked, and you clothed me: I was sick, and you visited me: I was in prison, and you came to me."

We are in this ministry, not for what we get out of it, not even because of what those to whom we witness get out of it. We do it because the Lord commands it; because He expects it. We do it for His sake..

GOD'S WILL

I have to say that sometimes I get a little tired of Christians who say they are waiting for God to show them what he wants them to do. What God wants is clear. He has already told us. "Go ye into all the world, and preach the gospel to every creature." Why are so many Christians waiting for a special message from God? The message has already been given to us all - "Preach the gospel."

Every day of the week I scour the newspapers and watch the television for information on big events taking place where I can witness. I'm looking for pop concerts, political rallies, football matches. Any place where there'll be crowds of human souls gathered. That's my mission field. That's my opportunity. Wherever there are crowds, I can raise my gospel banner and hand out tracts. That's my ministry. That's one way I can spread the good news of the gospel. Visiting the sick and the imprisoned is another.

Recently, the Prime Minister, John Major came to Dumfries. I saw this as a great opportunity to mount a witness for my Lord. The meeting was held in a large hall at the local hospital. As I climbed the hill on my mountain bike, packed with a bag of tracts, my gospel banner and jacket, telegram prayers were constantly ascending to Heaven.

"Please Lord, bind the spiritual forces of wickedness. Don't let them hinder me. Please give me good opportunities to witness. Please prevent self from trying to achieve what only You can achieve."

Those prayers were answered in a wonderful way. The banner was held high, many tracts were given out, and the jacket I wore, with gospel verses printed on it, also preached the Word powerfully. And there were a few bonuses. I was able to speak personally to three Government Ministers, Mr. Forsythe, Mr. Rifkind, Mr. Howard and - Mr. Major. On the news that evening my gospel banner was seen on every television station.

THE ELDER

As I press on in the faith it becomes more and more clear to me that the only thing that can change the hearts and minds of men and women is the Word of God. And the more I am involved in this witness the more I am appalled at the ignorance of people concerning the Scriptures.

I was giving out gospel tracts in the High Street one day when a smartly dressed gentleman approached. I proffered a tract in his direction. "Oh, I don't need that lad," he said, "I've been an elder in the church for thirty years."

"Oh well Sir," I replied, "Perhaps you'd be good enough to encourage me by giving me your testimony, telling me how you were born again."

"Born again! Born again!" he blustered. "Don't start giving me all that American jargon."

"But, it's God's own Word," I pointed out. "John chapter three. They're the words of Jesus. He spoke about the necessity of being born again."

"Don't try to convert me, sonny boy. I do my best." And he strode off down the street. How sad that even an elder of the church is unaware of the pure teaching of the Bible.

Why do people get so upset at a message that is so full of hope for mankind? And why do they get mad at me for proclaiming it? For years I brought nothing but misery and tears to those with whom I came into contact. I was a blight on society, a continual problem for the authorities, and a menace to everyone I met.

You would think they'd be delighted to see my life changed, and to see me out doing some good. Sadly, it's not always the case. A lot of people seem to hate me even more, now that I'm a Christian, than they did when I was wild and unruly.

DOING YOUR OWN THING

A man once approached me in the street and asked "Why do you stand here in the street all day with this banner? Why don't you ever go out and enjoy yourself?"

My reply was simple and straightforward. "Do you believe in doing your own thing?" I asked. He said that he did. "Then why is it that when I decide to do my own thing, standing here with this banner, you suspect me of not enjoying myself?"

"You mean, you like doing this?" he said in a rather startled voice. "Why yes, of course I do," I replied. "God has given me a love for the souls of men and women, and this is the way He wants me to reach them with the gospel. This is my thing, and I enjoy it."

When I thought more about it later, it came to mind that it's not really our own thing that matters, it's doing God's will. So many people want to do their own thing because they don't want to do God's thing. But the Bible tells us that "The will of God is good, and perfect, and acceptable." I've been much, much happier these last few years, doing God's will, than I ever was doing my own thing and getting into trouble for it.

IF ONLY!

As I come to the end of this book I find myself wondering why it ever had to be written. If I'd had the sense to listen to people wiser than I was, my life would have been so different. But then, the benefit of hindsight is wonderful, isn't it? I suppose most of us could say "if only," at some time or other. The past will always be with us, but we don't have to let it rule our lives.

I remember a policeman reprimanding me years ago. "You won't ever change your sort," he said. "People like you always stay the same. The leopard can't change it's spots. You are scum, and scum has to be flushed away."

Believe it or not, I understand how that guy felt. And if I'd been in his shoes I'd have said the same, I suppose. It's true, a leopard can't change its spots. But thank God for the one called Jesus who can take a poor sinner who was IMPOSSIBLE WITH MEN, and change him to such a degree that he has a purpose in life.

Now my life is filled with purpose. I have something to live for every day. And I've something to live for after I die. I wouldn't take anything the world has to offer to go back to my old ways. And all this as a result of God's great salvation.

Nothing in this world compares with the fellowship of the people I now keep company with - the people of God. I fellowship among the finest of people in our local Gospel Hall, in Dumfries. I have a lovely wife and daughter, and I have friends all over the world. But best of all - I have Jesus dwelling in my heart.

Chapter Twenty-Six

TURNAROUND

In closing, can I just say that you don't have to be in Berlinnie, Parkhurst, or San-Quentin to be in prison. People without Jesus in their hearts are prisoners of self. Don't continue to hide behind the locked door of your heart. Accept the finished work of Christ as being for you. Remember, He suffered, bled and died, descended into Hell, and arose again the victor, holding the key that can unlock the door of any heart. All you have to do is call upon his name. He waits for you ....

Bars on windows all around.
People lost and rarely found.
Always thinking of tomorrow,
One day less from pain and sorrow.

Hobbs and Co., S.E. 11.
Number of nuts fifty-seven.
Open your tin, roll a smoke.
You're only pleasure in the wing of no hope.

White Windsor! Is this a joke?
Our Queen's name on prison soap.
A thought bangs in "Better the Rope."
Chuck it out before you choke.

All night long - clang, clang, clang.
Wish it would stop - bang, bang, bang.
Muffled voices, cries of pain.
Some poor soul with an overload brain.

Slop out, exercise, Governor's request.
Shuffle along in line with the rest.
Shouting and bawling, jingling keys.
Oh for the outside, and a soft gentle breeze.

Remembering days as free as a bird.
The sun on your face, someone to love.
Now, here in bondage, a quick glance above.
Could Jesus help me and send the white Dove.

Forcing your mind not to accept
The reality of life, when there's no clock to set.
Your whole personality belonging to screws.
Your own soul your only good news.

Walking the yard with the rest of the fools.
Each one has broken all, or some rules.
Trying to believe you can take what they give.
Yet, deep down inside, you're struggling to live.

Take out your wrath on some weaker soul.
Kidding yourself you can handle the hole.
The truth is, you haven't got a friend
And your pride will rule you, right to the end.

Life passes on and you're trapped in the cage.
What finally happens to your bottle up rage?
In the end you let loose in some crazy way.
Then, it's grey walls and hate for the rest of your days.

Wise up my friend, you still have a chance.
Accept King Jesus and He'll make you dance.
The true God will glady take your poor soul.
He'll clean out your heart, make you strong and whole.

He does care, my friend, of that I am sure.
He'll love you forever, you'll never be poor.
So step out of darkness and pull off your mask.
Jesus died for your sins, both present and past.

God took your place in the form of a man.
He did it like this. Do you understand?
He died for us all, but it doesn't stop there.
You must trust Him and love Him. Will you dare?

You may say to yourself "Who's he to shout?"
Well I'll tell you. It's me this poem's about.
I'm one, who for years lay in the jail.
My life was empty and destined to fail.

After years of violence, in seventy-nine.
I begged Jesus spirit to come and be mine.
Because I was genuine He did as I said.
I constantly thank Him. I should have been dead.

Yes, I wish you good fortune, wherever you walk.
Please don't be like me and end up in the dock.
Call upon Him while you still have a chance.
He'll love you forever, your life enhance.

*Christ is the answer
to your need*